DATE DUE

			PRINTED IN U.S.A.

Responsi

Account

Responsible Management Accounting and Controlling

A Practical Handbook for Sustainability, Responsibility, and Ethics

Daniel A. Ette

BEP BUSINESS EXPERT PRESS

First published in 2015 by
Business Expert Press, LLC
222 East 46th Street, New York, NY 10017
www.businessexpertpress.com

ISBN-13: 978-1-60649-822-4 (paperback)
ISBN-13: 978-1-60649-823-1 (e-book)

Business Expert Press Principles of Responsible Management Education Collection

Collection ISSN: 2331-0014 (print)
Collection ISSN: 2331-0022 (electronic)

Cover and interior design by Exeter Premedia Services Private Ltd., Chennai, India

First edition: 2015

10 9 8 7 6 5 4 3 2 1

Printed in the United States of America.

This book is dedicated to all people who share my responsible controlling vision and especially to those who always supported me in writing down the idea of a controlling approach that positively fosters corporate responsibility and corporate sustainability. Many thanks also to the ones who challenged me in the process of bringing my ideas onto these papers. You have not been of less importance than the ones who gave me their support.

And, above all, thanks to Barbara and to the rest of my family!

Abstract

Sustainability is becoming a business megatrend. The issue of this book is to be seen in the fact that controlling departments are hardly involved in sustainability topics and do not contribute to corporate responsibility. This book postulates the following assertion: responsible controlling is indispensable to make an organization more responsible. The objective of this book is the conceptual development of a responsible controlling framework toward decision making which is based on an ethical fundament in order to make a company a responsible business.

This book presents a thoroughly examined recommended course of action regarding responsible controlling for practitioners based on a profound theoretical background. We take a close look onto responsibility. In this context we find out that responsibility means recognizing the unimpeachable freedom of all human beings. Corporate responsibility deals with the legitimate claims of all stakeholders. Ethics as a basis for responsibility must not be understood as one ethical approach in the realms of consequentialism or nonconsequentialism. Rather a prism of ethical theories helps to better understand the issue at hand. Especially Kant's categorical imperative, extended by a consequentialist view, is helpful.

I show what is to be understood by controlling in an organizational context and in which areas controllers are active. Moreover we will regard different controlling approaches toward sustainability. Yet, we realize that the prevalent controlling concepts are not sufficient with respect to responsibility.

Through the development of a responsible controlling framework I give recommendations how the status quo of controlling should be altered in terms of both tools and mindsets. In detail I elaborate a twelve-step responsible controlling roadmap which shows how controlling can contribute to foster a corporation's responsible behavior and how sustainability topics can be integrated in management decisions. With regard to decisions, I expose that the basis for good decisions is to be seen in the recognition of all legitimate claims and thus in the unimpeachable human dignity of all human beings. I do not provide a catalogue with clear-cut answers or behavioral instructions. On the contrary, it becomes evident, that ethics as a critical reflection effort is central to responsible controlling. Decisions in a responsible sense will not be made on hard facts, like profit, as the sole criterion. Soft facts must also be considered.

I conclude with the defense of my assertion. Responsible controlling must first and foremost be understood as a mindset. If controllers change their mindsets and their tools and encourage others to do so as well, I claim as a conclusion that responsible controlling is an uncommon but indispensable approach of making an organization more responsible.

Keywords

boundary, communication, controlling, corporate responsibility, corporate social performance, corporate social responsibility, creating shared value, data platform, decision making, dilemma situations, ethics, green controlling, key performance indicators, management accounting, materiality, mission, reporting for sustainability, responsibility, responsible controlling, responsible controlling framework, responsible controlling roadmap, scope, sociocontrolling, stakeholder, sustainability, sustainability controlling, targets, triple bottom line, vision

Contents

Responsible Controlling Vision

In responsible controlling the assumption of responsibility is deeply rooted in every controlling function. Controlling is a driver toward corporate responsibility and sustainability and focuses on positively influencing the triple bottom line. Ethics as a reflection effort is the basis for every action.

CHAPTER 1

Setting the Stage

"Nowadays people know the price of everything and the value of nothing."[1]

—Oscar Wilde

1.1 Why Read This Book

Sustainability is becoming a business megatrend that can no longer be ignored by managers.[2] More and more stakeholders consider the so-called externalities like water usage and pollution, as well as carbon dioxide emissions, as crucial elements of a company's performance. Moreover, globally interacting supply chains lead to environmental strains and also to corresponding liabilities of business actors. In the future, all parts of a business will be affected by sustainability-related issues.[3] A "clear vision and the (necessary) execution capabilities"[4] are crucial in order to be a pioneer within this megatrend.

In addition to the expression "sustainability," other terms like corporate social responsibility (CSR) or corporate responsibility (CR) are being discussed among academicians as well as in business environments.[5] Regarding CSR, Milton Friedman states in his article, *The Social Responsibility of Business Is to Increase its Profits*, that businesses cannot have responsibilities other than making profits.[6] But does that mean that profit maximization should be the overall goal of a corporation? Already Adam Smith, the founder of the market economy, considers the well-being of mankind as the central idea of economic activities,[7] and not profit maximization. Profit only is the yardstick

> Corporate Social Responsibility, Corporate Sustainability, or Corporate Responsibility: Same or Different?
>
> Our understanding will be clarified in Chapter 2—for the moment we will use the expressions as synonyms.

to measure the efficiency. In today's economy, though, profit has become an end in itself, while the production of goods and services only serves as a means to this end.[8]

Sustainability and CR matter not only in terms of environmental issues, but also in terms of social factors. They are not less important. In our current economic behavior, human rights are often infringed and people are only seen as a means to an end. Moreover, against the backdrop of the aging population in Europe and the resulting shortage of skilled labor, high-potentials increasingly look for employers who provide meaning and values within the job—a job in which the employees can contribute to the development of the society and have an adequate work–life balance.[9] As shown in the United Nations' *World Population Prospects*, in contrast to Europe the global population is rapidly growing.[10] As incomes internationally are expected to rise, resource consumption will also increase. Hence, corporations are acting in a field of expanding markets, while resources are running out and their prices becoming more volatile.[11]

There are many other aspects in which companies strive toward sustainability. It may be due to intensified customer interest in ecological products[12] or due to an increasing regulation in the field of CSR in many parts of the world. Furthermore, there is an increasing corporate obligation to legitimize its behavior in society and to adapt to a new understanding of a corporation's role.[13] Undoubtedly, corporations must contribute toward a sustainable development and not leave this task exclusively to the state and to society.[14] As a side effect, companies thereby have the chance to participate in scoping sustainable actions and not just having to react to legislative pressures. The United Nations Global Compact is one prominent example that defines 10 voluntary principles in the fields of human rights, labor practices, environment, and anticorruption with which companies should be compliant and give a guideline for responsible behavior (Table 1.1).[15]

Being sustainable means that all parts of a business must necessarily be integrated into the strive for sustainable development. The finance departments too need to realize the relevance of these global issues. An Ernst & Young survey, conducted in 2011, shows six trends on sustainability in a business environment. Among them, three directly influence

Table 1.1 The 10 principles of the United Nations Global Compact

Field		Principle
Human rights	1	Businesses should support and respect the protection of internationally proclaimed human rights; and
	2	make sure that they are not complicit in human rights abuses.
Labor	3	Businesses should uphold the freedom of association and the effective recognition of the right to collective bargaining;
	4	the elimination of all forms of forced and compulsory labor;
	5	the effective abolition of child labor; and
	6	the elimination of discrimination in respect of employment and occupation.
Environment	7	Businesses should support a precautionary approach to environmental challenges;
	8	undertake initiatives to promote greater environmental responsibility; and
	9	encourage the development and diffusion of environmentally friendly technologies.
Anticorruption	10	Businesses should work against corruption in all of its forms, including extortion and bribery.

Source: United Nations (2000).

an organization's finance section: (1) sustainability reporting is growing but currently is not well equipped; (2) the chief financial officer (CFO) is gaining an important role; and (3) sustainability rankings and ratings are becoming relevant to business leaders.[16]

In this book, the question is raised whether and how the management accounting and controlling function can contribute toward fostering a corporation's responsible behavior.

Facts

Sixty-six percent of the respondents of the Ernst & Young survey realize a growing number of sustainability-related inquiries from investors and shareholders. Therefore, the need for reporting is growing.

Thirty-nine percent of the respondents stress the importance of the CFO because of his or her role in approving the budget for sustainability topics.

Ernst and Young (2012).

Moreover, it will be examined if a responsibly behaving controlling department is necessary and useful for organizations.

The book postulates the assertion that **responsible controlling is indispensable to make an organization more responsible.** The core issues addressed in this book are that finance and controlling departments are barely involved in sustainability topics and that they do not contribute to CR, as shown in the *Corporate Sustainability Barometer* published in 2010.[17] Against the backdrop of the global megatrends, management accounting and controlling must detach itself from being driven only by monetary issues. There is a need for controlling to make a greater contribution in terms of responsible behavior by extending the company's instruments toward nonmonetary criteria and also by changing controlling's mindset toward a more responsible and joint thinking. With the aim of rendering assistance to this effort, the book elaborates on a controlling framework that should help foster an organization's responsibility. While attempting this we should always bear in mind that "nowadays people know the price of everything and the value of nothing."[18] What Oscar Wilde expressed more than 100 years ago is still a valid claim.

Facts

Controlling departments are hardly involved in sustainability topics. *Eight percent* of the interviewees see finance, controlling, and accounting as supportive for sustainability matters. Whereas *89.3 percent* of the respondents consider public relations and communications as beneficial for sustainability.

Schaltegger, Windolph, and Harms (2010).

1.2   What Are the Objectives of This Book

Claim

Responsible controlling is not only about new tools. Mindset changes are indispensable when it comes to a new understanding of controlling.

Considering the current global economic and social pitfalls, there is a need for more responsible corporations. In their survey, *The Limits to Growth*, conducted for the Club of Rome in 1972, Meadow and colleagues point out that it is the will of humankind that is crucial for a prevailing and effective sustainable behavior.[19] The fact that sustainability nowadays is perceived as a megatrend consequently arises from a will in society and from a change in peoples' mindset toward a socially and ecologically responsible world.[20] For the effort of establishing a responsible controlling framework, it means that changes in mindset are indispensable when it comes to current tasks and motivations of controlling.

According to Schaltegger, Windolph, and Harms, the awareness of sustainability has reached the top-level management of corporations.[21] But how can this awareness be broken down and integrated into different corporate functions? Unlike specialized departments for CSR and unlike many corporate communications departments, finance and controlling is currently less involved in sustainability topics. Even more alarming is the fact that only eight percent of the respondents of the *Corporate Sustainability Barometer* consider finance and controlling as having a positively fostering influence on sustainability.[22] Hence, controlling is not perceived as being a driver toward sustainability. This is to be seen as a serious integration deficit. The original task of controlling—providing information to the management in order to facilitate the decision making process—is not performed adequately when it comes to sustainability. Given the relevance of sustainability that is surprising. As a consequence, corporations miss the opportunity to use established information and management approaches and neglect the integration of sustainability and finance information.[23]

I have worked in a controlling function for several years. Moreover, I have been highly involved in establishing controlling practices that do not only consider monetary factors while decision making. This circumstance, together with the aforementioned social and environmental issues, led to the motivation of and the following discussions in this book:

- It shall be evaluated and shown whether and how controlling (departments) can contribute toward fostering a corporation's responsible behavior.
- Can controlling be a driver toward corporate sustainability and can sustainability topics be integrated in management decisions?
- And what should be the basis for good decisions?

To answer these questions, a look at ethical thinking will help.

According to Crane and Matten, business ethics is concerned with "business situations ... and *decisions* (italics added) where issues of (morally) right and wrong are addressed."[24] Hence, I raise the question why there shouldn't be a link between ethics and controlling. After all, both are concerned with decision making. Last but not least it is to ask how adequate controlling tools could look like and how controllers' mindset and thinking would need to change. In short: How can such a "responsible controlling" be implemented?

The objective of this book is the conceptual development of a responsible controlling framework toward decision making, which is based on an ethical principle in order to make a company a responsible business. It can be assumed that it will be a difficult path to integrate ethical thinking into actual controlling behavior and to make responsibility a cornerstone in controlling. However, I am convinced that responsible controlling can contribute a lot to foster an organization's responsible behavior. Therefore, within this book, a recommended course of action for practitioners based on a profound theoretical background for academic readers will be developed. The intention is to inform management accounting practice and help current and future business leaders navigate through the topic of responsible business from a controlling perspective.

1.3   Structure of This Book and Who Should Read It

At the beginning, the context and the relevance of the issue of responsible controlling has been detailed. The following chapters will be concerned with the theoretical foundations of (1) responsibility, sustainability, and ethics (RSE; Chapter 2); (2) management accounting and controlling (Chapter 3); and (3) controlling sustainability and responsibility (Chapter 4). Regarding responsibility, we will examine what is to be understood by responsibility in an organizational context. Furthermore, you will find a discussion on why your organization should assume responsibility, which responsibilities should be taken into account, and for whom an organization is responsible.

Chapters 5, 6, and 7 synthesize responsibility and controlling and set up responsible controlling. To do so, a responsible controlling framework and a roadmap have been developed. Within the roadmap, there are recommendations on how to establish controlling as a driver toward sustainability. Finally, Chapter 8 summarizes all the topics discussed previously.

This book may be valuable for you, if you are

- a student or a professor in a business school or an MBA and an executive MBA student and like to get introduced to tangible but uncommon thinking from a controlling perspective;
- a practitioner within the field of controlling and management accounting and you are assigned to install a controlling system which takes into account RSE;
- a practitioner within the field of CR or corporate sustainability and you need to get familiar with the topic of steering a corporation;
- a corporate executive and you would like to make your organization both successful and a pioneer in sustainability.

1.4   How to Read This Book

Of course, it makes sense to read the entire book. However, if your time is limited there are different approaches to read through this book, depending on your intentions and your state of knowledge.

You would probably benefit from reading the entire book if you are

- a student in business school or an MBA and executive MBA student and you are not yet familiar with the topics of RSE or with controlling;
- a professor in business school and you would like to teach not only the current mainstream management accounting and controlling practices but also some alternative approaches;
- a practitioner within the field of controlling and management accounting and you are assigned to install a controlling system that takes into account RSE and you do not have enough insights into these topics yet.

If you are a practitioner in the field of controlling, and you already have knowledge in terms of RSE, you may directly read the responsible controlling framework (Chapters 5, 6 and 7). If you are a practitioner within the field of CR and you need to get familiar with the topic of steering a corporation it would be helpful for you to start reading Chapter 3. As a corporate executive who likes to steer his or her organization successfully under the conditions of RSE you may at least have a look at the responsible controlling framework (Chapters 5, 6, and 7) in order to get an idea how to integrate responsible behavior into traditional corporate management.

1.5   Some Points to Remember

Sustainability is becoming a business megatrend that should no longer be ignored by managers and by controlling departments—that is, by you. In future, all parts of a business will be affected by sustainability. Finance and controlling must make its contribution. Therefore, ask yourself and your team: Why should profit maximization (not) be the ultimate goal of a corporation and thus (not be) an end in itself?

However, currently finance and controlling departments are hardly involved in sustainability topics and do not contribute toward CR. The original task of controlling—providing information to the management to facilitate the decision making process—is not performed in an adequate manner when it comes to sustainability. Therefore, there is a need for controlling to make a greater contribution in terms of responsible behavior by extending the company's instruments toward nonmonetary criteria and also by changing the mindset toward a more responsible and joint thinking.

In an effort to make an organization more sustainable, responsible controlling is indispensable. Therefore, this book provides a recommended course of action for practitioners regarding responsible controlling based on a profound theoretical background. The intention is to inform about management accounting practice and help current and future business leaders navigate through the topic of responsible business from a controlling perspective.

CHAPTER 2

Responsibility, Sustainability, and Ethics

"I believe that every right implies a responsibility; every opportunity an obligation; every possession, a duty."[1]

—John D. Rockefeller Jr.

ResCoCo—An Example That Will Accompany Us

Imagine you are a corporate management accountant in a medium-sized company, called Responsible Controlling Company, *ResCoCo*. The company produces different consumer goods and therefore also needs many purchase products. The market in which ResCoCo is active is a very competitive one. The corporate culture, however, is to be described as a pleasurable one and the management board normally strives to reconcile the interests of the owners and the employees. In the past you have been involved in many accounting projects. Your latest project now is to introduce sustainable and responsible thinking into the controlling department and into the whole company.

Ethical Issues Are Not That Far

In the past year, the company has not been very successful. Owing to that the management board has asked you to set up a plan on how to make the company's financial bottom line more resilient. Not seeing another solution, they say there are no taboos. After screening all the available data and reports, you find out that one of the corporate divisions is not profitable. You assume the reason is to be seen in an outdated product range. From a mere financial perspective you would suggest to the management board that the division should be sold or dissolved. However, your close friend is a middle manager in this division. If you make your suggestion, your friend would be laid off. And that is not all. She has a family with two kids and has just bought a house.

Now you are probably in the middle of a real ethical dilemma! How would you decide? And how would you decide if she would not have been a close friend of yours but only an anonymous person? Would you suggest to the management board to sell the division or not?

Another solution may be to reduce costs of sourced goods. Together with the head of the purchasing department you found another supplier for your main purchased good. The costs could be reduced significantly. However, industry insiders claim that this supplier does not take care of his employees. The supplier itself does not give you any information on labor contracts. Moreover, some NGOs revealed a big environmental scandal in which this supplier was one of the main characters.

What would you do in this case? Either changing the supplier and making sure that your company can continue to exist in its entirety? In this case you would accept environmental and human rights infringements. Or rather laying off some of your internal staff?

2.1   Responsibility and Sustainability in an Organizational Context

2.1.1   Responsibility—Setting the Stage

In the introduction of this book, I have used the terms of corporate sustainability and corporate (social) responsibility in an exchangeable way. In this chapter, we examine different definitions in order to understand them thoroughly and set the stage for further in-depth elaborations.

First, we take a general look at the term *responsibility*. According to the Oxford Dictionaries, *being responsible* means "having an obligation to do something, or having control over or care for someone."[2] More precisely, it says that responsibility involves important duties and independent decision making.[3] As regards to duty, they understand the duty to report to superiors and to be "answerable to them for one's actions."[4] Moreover, *being responsible* means, for them, that one is "capable of being trusted" and "morally accountable for one's behavior."[5] Within this definition of the Oxford Dictionaries, different terms—like duties, control, decision making, and moral—are rolled into one term: responsibility. Hence, there is no clear-cut definition of responsibility provided, which could be used to make the term clearer for you. One may even ask if having control over others and being accountable is not a contradiction. Later, I question if *independent* decision making really is an attribute of responsibility and if it is a responsibility to have control over others.

However, it is to note, that (1) responsibility has to do with interconnections toward others, (2) there is a moral dimension included in being responsible, and (3) duties and trust are involved. Trustworthiness is to be understood as not being opportunistic.[6] That means that the trust someone is placing in you or in your company[7] must not be abused.[8] The retention of trustworthiness is depicted by Suchanek as the actual core of a corporation's responsibility.[9]

> Within this book I use the terms organization, corporation, company, and firm as synonyms.

2.1.2   Corporate Social Responsibility

Since controlling is related to an organizational framework—not being a private matter—we examine what is assumed as *corporate* (social) responsibility within the established literature. In his 1979 article, Carroll states that the "social responsibility of business encompasses the economic, legal, ethical, and discretionary expectations that society has of organizations at a given point of time."[10] The Commission of the European Communities defines in 2001 that CSR is a "concept whereby companies integrate social and environmental concerns in their business operations and in their interaction with their stakeholders on a voluntary basis."[11]

The *integration into the business operations* makes CSR distinct from corporate philanthropy. Philanthropy as "the desire to promote the welfare of others, expressed especially by the generous donation of money to good causes"[12] does not necessarily have anything to do with the business processes themselves. The common ground of CSR and philanthropy,

Corporate Social Responsibility deals voluntarily with the integration of environmental and social topics into the *core* business processes. It should not be confused with pure philanthropy. Rather, it addresses the company's actual way of doing business. Stakeholder thinking—as opposed to mere shareholder orientation—is a central concern for CSR.

however, is to be seen in the voluntariness that the European Commission claims. Derived from that point, it can be stated that CSR is dealing with environmental and societal issues "over and above . . . legal obligations."[13] Carroll also includes the legal aspects into CSR.[14] Within its new definition of 2011, the European Commission defines CSR as "the responsibility of enterprises for their impacts on society,"[15] for which respecting laws and agreements with social partners is a necessary precondition. To assume CSR, not only environmental and social, but also consumer concerns, human rights, and ethical issues should be integrated into the corporations' operations and core strategy "in close collaboration with their stakeholders."[16] The aim is to create shared value for both owners or shareholders and other stakeholders.[17] The concept of *creating shared value* will be discussed in Chapter 4.

One more recent attempt to define (corporate) social responsibility on a global stage is the International Organization for Standardization (ISO) 26000 standard.[18] In its introduction, the ISO states that the "objective of social responsibility is to contribute to sustainable development."[19] Obviously, there is a connection between social responsibility and sustainability. Consequently, we discuss the term *sustainability* within this chapter. But, prior to this discussion, let us take a look at the ISO 26000 definition. It is to mention that the ISO does not talk about CSR but only about "social responsibility"[20] since not only corporations should be addressed but also all types of organizations. According to the ISO, an organization has a responsibility "for the **impacts** . . . of its decisions and activities on society and the **environment** . . . through transparent and **ethical behaviour.**"[21]

This behavior

- is conducive to a sustainable development;
- deals with stakeholders' expectations;

- is compliant to applicable law and to internationally recognized behavioral norms; and
- is integrated into the whole organization and its relationships.[22]

At this stage, we could have a look at a lot more definitions. But even taking only the aforestated sources—Carroll, the European Commission, and the ISO—into account, it is already evident to you that just as for *responsibility*, there is no precise definition for *CSR*. Accordingly, Garriga and Melé mention that CSR is a field of complex, unclear, and controversial approaches and different theories.[23] Crane and Matten state that "CSR . . . still remains a relatively vague and in many respects arbitrary construct."[24] Although the term CSR has become part of mainstream, and the scientific community is concerned with it, there is no uniform definition and no accurate distinction to other terms. Even the aforementioned, internationally recognized ISO 26000, which has done a lot to foster organizational responsibility, has not solved that problem. This imprecise understanding of CSR leads to disappointment both among the business world and within the civil society since different expectations are aroused. According to Schneider, *making a final definition of CSR is not possible.*[25] CSR is a dynamic "moving issue,"[26] which is performed distinctly. The implementation depends on the different core processes of different types of organizations. However, the question can be raised if a clear-cut definition is necessary at all or if it is even conducive against the backdrop of a concept like CSR, which is based on a continuous improvement process.[27]

2.1.3 Sustainability

The ambiguity of CSR leads us to another term: *sustainability.* Sustainability or sustainable development is related to CSR. The fundamental principles of both concepts are overlapping. Remember, for example, the ISO 26000 states that the "objective of social responsibility is to contribute to sustainable development."[28] However, the question is, what is sustainability? Already back in the seventeenth century, Hannß Carl von Carlowitz claims that in terms of a sustainable forestry only as many trees

Sustainability in the corporate arena means ensuring that all processes and tasks are conducted in such a way that there are at least no negative impacts—maybe even positive ones—on environment and society. Current and future generations must not be negatively influenced by our corporate decisions. That can be called corporate sustainability.

must be cut down as can grow again within the same period of time.[29] Von Carlowitz mentions that the mining industry cuts down too many forests and notices that the clearing of the trees must be limited in order to make sure that wood can serve as a raw material for the mining industry in the years to come. Hence, the economic survival of the mining industry is an important aspect for von Carlowitz. In addition, the economy has to serve the society and therefore has a duty to not exploit nature.[30] Nearly 300 years later the World Commission on Environment and Development of the United Nations defines sustainable development in its so-called Brundtland Report as development,

> which implies meeting the needs of the present without compromising the ability of future generations to meet their own needs.[31]

The Brundtland Report contains two central statements: sustainable development needs to consider *intergenerational justice* and *intragenerational justice*. Intergenerational justice (see von Carlowitz) means that today's generations should only behave in a way that future generations have similar opportunities to shape their own lives. Intragenerational justice, which is often neglected in the sustainability discussion, implies that the (good and bad) consequences of today's economic behavior should also be shared equally within and between countries. In other words, the "environmental costs and benefits of economic development"[32] should be borne equally both between today's world population and between today's and the future generations.

While one may question if *social* responsibility comprises the striving for adequate environmental behavior, others may ask if the Brundtland definition only aims at "sustainable and environmentally sound development,"[33] without taking a social dimension into consideration. That is not the case. However, in 1992, the United Nations further defined the term sustainable development in its conference on environment and development in Rio, Brazil. Principle 1 of its *Rio Declaration on Environment and Development* states that,

> human beings are at the centre of concerns for sustainable development. They are entitled to a healthy and productive life in harmony with nature.[34]

Thus, obviously, a sound environment has to go hand in hand with an awareness of social issues. However, remembering von Carlowitz as the founder of the term sustainability,[35] the economic survival (of companies or states) is crucial as well. Russ states that "sustainability in the end is a means of conducting environmentally sound economic activity for socially desirable outcomes."[36] Economic survival and sound economic activity, however, are not equal to profit maximization. That leads us to the next relevant term within this book: the *triple bottom line*.

2.1.4   Triple Bottom Line

To make the notion of sustainability more concrete—also for companies—Elkington introduces the so-called triple bottom line approach of sustainability.[37] But what is to be understood by the triple bottom line? The Cambridge Dictionaries explain *bottom line* as "the total profit or loss of a company at the end of a particular period of time."[38] Hence, in the common usage, the term bottom line is an economic one and is associated with money, more precisely with "the total profit or loss"[39] of the profit and loss account. Elkington expands this view by introducing two more dimensions: a social and an environmental. This triad—also known as people, planet, and profit—is called triple bottom line.[40] In other words, economic, ecological, and social factors need to be aligned and should be tantamount. The triple bottom line should measure the value added that a company creates with respect to the economic, ecological, and social dimension.[41] It "captures the essence of sustainability by measuring the impact of an organization's activities on the world."[42] Later in this book, we look at how to measure triple bottom line issues within an organizational context. At this point, it is to say that critics argue that the benefit of social activities cannot be measured as exactly as the profit.[43] The same also applies to environmental issues. What is, for example, an organization's effect on biodiversity?

Nevertheless, if intra- and intergenerational justice should be achieved, the current impact must not be negative. Hence, a sustainable business must conduct its processes in such a way that at least a neutral impact on environment and society is ensured in accordance with a sound economic performance. Sound economic performance in this context is not a precisely defined term and may depend on the sector and the country in which an organization acts. However, it is not to be understood as profit maximization. Corporations behave sustainably if all processes of the value chain are performed well against the backdrop of the triple bottom line.[44] In terms of sustainability, Barbier uses a Venn diagram of intersecting circles (Figure 2.1): only in the overlap of economy, ecology, and society, a sustainable development is possible.[45]

Earlier, I have shown that there is no precise definition of CSR. Pezzey makes the following statement after having tried to find a definition for sustainability for several years: "So I see little point in expanding the collection of fifty sustainability definitions which I made in 1989, to the five thousand definitions that one could readily find today."[46] This shows that we will not be able to find a unique definition for sustainability as well. However, the Brundtland Report, the Rio Declaration, and the triple bottom line notion give us some reference points on a global scale. To establish a working definition within this book, I summarize the basic factors

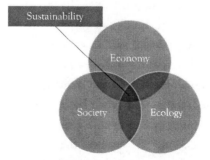

Figure 2.1 Barbier's Venn diagram of sustainability

Source: Barbier (1987). © 1987 Foundation for Environmental Conservation. Adapted with the permission of Cambridge University Press.

of CSR and sustainability. Based on a set of attributes that cannot clearly be allocated to either CSR or corporate sustainability, I will continue to use the two terms (corporate) sustainability and corporate (social) responsibility interchangeably within this book. Sustainability, finally, may not be exclusively reached by corporations and it is a bigger picture than CSR. Sustainability can only be achieved if society and politics contribute as well. In this book I focus on the corporate aspects.

2.1.5   Some Points to Remember

As discussed earlier, corporate (social) responsibility and corporate sustainability

- are related to the integration of responsibility into the business operations and its core strategy;
- are conducted on a voluntary basis, over and above legal requirements;
- are concerned with stakeholders;
- deal with intragenerational and intergenerational justice; and
- take into account the triple bottom line approach, which means the balance of the three dimensions of sustainability: society, economy, and ecology.

2.2   Why Should an Organization Assume Responsibility—Profit or Morality? An Uncommon Discussion in a Management Book

So far, we have figured out that it is difficult to define responsibility in an unequivocal manner. Nevertheless, two basic terms used with respect to responsible corporate behavior have been introduced: corporate social responsibility and corporate sustainability. However, one important question is left open up to now: **Why should a company assume responsibility at all**? Further, I raise this question and give distinct answers. One term that was named in the previous chapter but was not further defined should help us in this endeavor: **ethics**—an uncommon word in a management book, but not to be underestimated when it comes to CSR and corporate sustainability. But, before having a look at ethics, let us start by answering the question from the headline of this chapter by considering some statements of a famous economist.

Nobel laureate Milton Friedman answers why a company should assume responsibility by stating that "there is one and only one social responsibility of business . . . (and that is) to increase its profits so long as it stays within the rules of the game."[47] With this, he generally denies any corporate responsibility in terms of social and environmental aspects that go over and above regulations and laws—the only valid liability is to generate as much profit as possible. Friedman explains his statement by arguing with the principal–agent relationship. A corporate executive is only an agent of the company owners (who are the principals). The main responsibility of the manager, therefore, is to meet the owners' expectations. If the executive took social responsibilities of the corporation itself into account, he would deprive the owners of their right to freely choose their profit utilization.[48] Moreover, Friedman talks about a "cloak of social responsibility,"[49] meaning that CSR actions are conducted in order to achieve other long-term goals under the guise of social responsibility. These could be, for example, being attractive to future employees or achieving a good image. Garriga and Melé make a classification in which Friedman's approach could be classified as an instrumental one.[50] Within this instrumental view, CSR is used strategically only "to achieve economic objectives and, ultimately, wealth creation."[51]

Obviously, there are many motives for making sustainability a topic within your company. Tschandl sees five motives when it comes to sustainable economic behavior:[52] (1) risk reduction and risk management, (2) chances for innovation and differentiation, (3) improved productivity, (4) stakeholder orientation, and (5) legitimation and acceptance.

Out of these five motivations, the first three can clearly be allocated to Friedman's view and, hence, to instrumentalism. The terms *stakeholder orientation* and *legitimation and acceptance* give the impression that there

Think Outside the Box

What are the motives why

- your company
- your controlling department
- you personally

should engage in a more responsible behavior?

may also be noninstrumental factors that could be relevant. These factors, which are not purely economic ones, may be seen in moral reasons, as opposed to a mere instrumental justification of CSR. For example, environmental and social problems that are caused by an organization, such as air pollution, should also be remedied by the company. From an ethical or moral perspective, the corporation has the responsibility to solve the arising problems.[53] Think about acid rain or respiratory diseases. Yet, we will see that building up corporate behavior only on *acceptance* is not a valid moral argument when it comes to the question why a corporation should assume responsibility. While I have shown five motives, several more could be found when we consider why corporations are interested in sustainability.

At this point, you may ask yourself: What are the motives why my company, my controlling department, or I personally should engage in a more responsible behavior? In general, we can define two impetuses for CSR: first, the so-called business case for CSR and, second, an ethical understanding as the basis for corporate behavior.

2.2.1 The Business Case for CSR

A business case is generally "a justification for a proposed project or undertaking on the basis of its expected commercial benefit."[54] In the context of this chapter it means the justification for dealing with sustainability issues on the basis of expected positive contributions to the company's survival and its financial bottom line. The question for the business case is: How can my company reap a benefit from a responsible behavior? Willard, for example, identifies seven benefits for corporations with regard to the business case for sustainability or CSR[55]:

- Increased revenue and market share
- Reduced energy expenses
- Reduced waste expenses
- Reduced materials and water expenses
- Increased employee productivity
- Reduced hiring and attrition expenses
- Reduced risks.

Especially the first and the last point could be justified with the following exemplary causal chain.

Think Outside the Box

Make a list of which actions, products, or processes within your company (or a company of interest) contribute positively or negatively to an assumed business case for sustainability.

How could you align social responsibility and your own corporate success?

From a global perspective, there is an unbelievably great amount of ecological and social problems. Different parts of the world move together by installing worldwide operating supply chains, which have big negative ecological and partly social impacts. Simultaneously, we face an increasing world population. As a result, resource scarcity, climate change, and allocation problems (for example, access to drinking water) are becoming more and more prevalent and are coming into the public focus. Hence, the topic of corporate responsibility becomes more tangible for many customers. This interest is also driven by the possibility of getting real-time information of nearly every issue or crisis, thanks to the better worldwide transparency that the Internet enables. Parts of the population and customer segments realize these global issues and exert pressure onto the corporate realm—for example, through their purchasing behavior and consumption patterns. They demand that corporations contribute positively to solving these problems. This means, it is more and more expected that companies assume responsibility. Companies that are sustainability pioneers in their field could *increase their market shares and raise their profits*. Moreover, they could *reduce the risk* of negative customer perception. Within the business community, these economic chances and necessities, accompanying the depicted pressure, are very often the first contact to sustainability.

Regarding the aforementioned business case points of reduced energy, reduced waste, and reduced expenses on materials and water, corporate sustainability is understood as allocating resources in a better way. Here, efficiency is the catchphrase: a more efficient usage of resources is good (or at least less bad) for the environment *and* is simultaneously good for the company's bottom line.

Good and Questionable Real-Life Corporate Sustainability Examples

The Good Example

Vaude—The Spirit of Mountain Sports[56]

Vaude is one of the leading outdoor equipment suppliers in Europe. Its aim until 2015 is to become Europe's most sustainable outdoor brand. The company has received many different awards for its activities in the past. Many products you can buy from Vaude are climate neutral. First, the emissions within the production process are cut down to a minimum. The nonavoidable emissions are set off with well-known partner organizations. Also in the social realm Vaude keeps pace with time. The company is a member of the Fair Wear Foundation, a multistakeholder initiative that strives for fair and improved working conditions in low-wage countries. The company is not pursuing an approach that only sees sustainability as a business and nothing else. Rather, it is obviously successful since it integrates responsible thinking into core processes. If you want to dig deeper, browse the company's responsibility site on the homepage: http://www.vaude.com/en-GB/Responsibility/

The Questionable Example

BP—"Beyond Petroleum"—Not anymore![57]

"Beyond Petroleum"—once BP's catchphrase to indicate that one of the world's largest energy companies goes its way toward renewable energies and to publically mitigate the Deepwater Horizon Disaster in 2010. However, in 2011, the company decided to exit solar power. In 2013, the company announced that it is divesting its wind power facilities. So what is left from "beyond petroleum"? Not much! Obviously, the sustainability track did not pay off. The sustainability business case BP looked for did not exist for the company. Being "a focused oil and gas company that creates value for shareholders by growing long-term sustainable free cash flow"[58] does (a) infringe the sustainability understanding of the Brundtland Report and (b) shows that BP is not willing to adapt its core business processes toward sustainable and responsible thinking.

The business case question is not per se reprehensible. At this point, one may argue that merely pursuing the business case for sustainability is probably not enough in the narrow sustainability sense, for example, with regard to postgrowth scenarios. Ultimately, it is necessary to act within the natural boundaries of our earth. A corporation that only contributes as long as a profit can be reaped may not be doing enough to reach this goal. Nevertheless, the more arguments exist for a business case, the less probable it is that corporations simply deny their social responsibility by arguing that they lose profit. Hence, the business case *could* enhance the chance for CSR measures to get implemented.[59] However, we must realize that the business case for sustainability—that is, the connection of moral claims and economic success—always has to meet economic requirements besides the moral ones. If these requirements cannot be met, the business case in the sense that striving for sustainability adds up to a better profit margin will not work and responsibility will probably not be overtaken entirely. However, *economic requirements* must not mean profit maximization, which leads to the following question: **Should there be other impetuses for organizations to assume responsibility?**

Taking again the definition of the ISO 26000 into account, an organization has a responsibility "for the **impacts** . . . of its decisions and activities . . . through transparent and **ethical behaviour**."[60] But you may wonder what ethical behavior actually is. Garriga and Melé mention a group of CSR theories that is concerned with ethics, which is "based on principles that express the right thing to do or the necessity to achieve a good society."[61] In the following sections, we will look at the second impetus for CSR (the ethical understanding) and the question why a company has responsibilities or should assume responsibility at all. We approach this issue from different ethical perspectives. First, we consider what is to be understood by (business) ethics. Later, we present some prevalent ethical theories. Within these theories, it will be evaluated if responsibility is and should be grounded on morality. Or if there may be ethically neutral spheres and thus corporations may not have responsibilities at all. This finding would mean seeing CSR only as an instrument for making more profit and hence would argue for the business case.

2.2.2   Ethics as a Basis for Responsible Action

Many people are not accustomed to the expression ethics. We therefore seek to clarify the field in order to arrive at a common understanding on which the responsible controlling framework can be based on.

Ethics deals with the correct action of individuals, which means *doing the right things*.[62] Ethics is a reflection effort.[63] It copes with the ultimately decisive, fundamental principles that *should* guide our acting. At this point, the question is: Have you ever reflected why you and your controlling department are behaving in the manner you do? And, have you asked which are the fundamental principles that guide your controlling action? Maybe profit maximization, maybe something else!

Imagine you being the controller of the ResCoCo example (see the box at the beginning of Chapter 2): you had figured out two options: (1) either laying off staff, including your friend or (2) changing the supplier and accepting environmental and human rights problems. In balancing the two different options, you are directly in the middle of an ethical reflection effort—without realizing it!

Think Outside the Box

If you have ever wondered what ethics has to do with you personally: Take some time and critically reflect your day-to-day behavior!

Do you think your private and corporate actions are perceived as being fair, responsible, or legitimate?

Yes ☐   No ☐

Dig Deeper

There are international organizations that concentrate on the promotion and the issues of business ethics. For example, have a look at the following websites:

Society for Business Ethics (www.sbeonline.org)

European Business Ethics Network (www.eben-net.org).

Both organizations hold conferences, publish latest articles, and spread the word of ethics in business.

While we have talked about the correct action of you as an individual so far, one may also raise the question of correct business actions.

Think Outside the Box

When you judge commercial, strategic, or financial situations of your corporation, do you take moral issues into account?

At this point, the subject of business ethics comes into play. Crane and Matten argue that "business ethics is the study of business situations, activities, and decisions where issues of (morally) right and wrong are addressed."[64] They emphasize that right and wrong are meant in a moral sense, "as opposed to . . . commercially, strategically, or financially right or wrong."[65] As a business person, you may pause for a moment and think about that statement. When you have been judging commercial, strategic, or financial situations of your corporation, have you taken into account or realized some moral issues in the past?

Integrative Economic Ethics

- perceives ethics as the inherent basis for every economic action;
- does not understand the economy as an ethically neutral sphere; and
- critically reflects the actual way of doing business.

Yet, how is the relationship of ethics and business? Ulrich talks about *integrative* economic ethics whereof business ethics is one part.[66,67] According to Ulrich, it is the purpose of economic ethics to fundamentally reassess the questionable relationship between the economy and ethical rationality.[68] Integrative economic ethics, in contrast to many applied ethics approaches, does *not* perceive ethics and the economy as opponents. The prevalent, "(mis-) understanding of economic ethics as *applied* ethics"[69] is based on the presumption that economic behavior is regarded as ethically neutral. In an applied ethical sense, ethics is an obstacle against being economically successful. Integrative economic ethics, by contrast, can be understood as "a critical reflection on the foundations of the normative *conditions* of economic rationality."[70] Thus, it critically reflects the actual way of doing business. As ResCoCo's controller, hence, you should fundamentally examine closer if the entire way of doing business is good or bad. Not only having a look at the current urgent case but also critically considering the whole company with its product range.

Dig Deeper: Moral and Morality

Moral is the sum of all de facto norms and principles that arrange an adequate acting within a specific cultural sphere and that are compulsory for everybody.[71] It is defining what one is allowed and what one is not allowed to do within a community. Moral norms are highly dependent on the acceptance of these norms within the community you are living in. However, this acceptance must not be confused with legitimacy on the basis of rational validity.

Morality is to be seen in the respect of the human claim toward itself to see oneself as a free subject.[72] This includes that human beings can deliberately give their view on themselves. The basis for morality is the *unimpeachable freedom* of all persons involved. The recognition of the claim of being a free subject is the fundamental moral condition of all *legitimate claims* that we could have toward other persons.[73]

Up until now I have given a first overview of what is meant by ethics. Basically it is about critical reflection. Moreover, the ones who have dug deeper have seen what is to be understood as moral and morality. The further elaborations within this book will be based on *morality*[74] as recognizing the unimpeachable freedom of all persons involved.

However, we have not been able to figure out what **ethical behaviour,**[75] as mentioned in the ISO standard, exactly means or what Carroll understands as the "ethical . . . expectations that society has of organizations at a given point of time."[76] Ulrich argues that modern ethics is rational ethics.[77] Such modern, discursive ethics does not simply apply norms out of a catalog, but asks how to deal with "conflicting values and interests" as well.[78] The underlying question of a modern business ethics is: **How would businesses have to behave in order to classify them as legitimate and responsible?** Another important question is why corporations should behave in this manner. While the first question (*how to*

Think Outside the Box

Have you ever questioned your actual way of doing business?

- How do you treat employees, customers, or other partners?
- How good or bad is your environmental behavior?

behave) has already partly been addressed previously in the text (see corporate social responsibility, sustainability, and the triple bottom line thinking) the latter (*why*) will be discussed subsequently. We consider two different ethical theories. Crane and Matten talk, among others, about consequentialist and nonconsequentialist ethical theories.[79] These theories should guide us toward possible answers to *why* a company should engage in responsible behavior.

2.2.3   Consequentialist Ethics

Consequentialist ethics approaches "address right and wrong according to the outcomes of a decision."[80] There are different viewpoints regarding these outcomes. Crane and Matten call the underlying approaches *egoism* and *utilitarianism*. In egoism, "an action is morally right if the decision-maker freely decides in order to pursue either their (short-term) desires or their (long-term) interests."[81] The second is the utilitarianist approach, which some see as one of the prevalent ethical approaches in the Western English-speaking world.[82] Utilitarianism can be classified as teleology, derived from the word *goal* in the Greek language.[83] Within utilitarianism (made popular by Bentham and Mill), "an action is morally right if it results in the greatest amount of good for the greatest amount of people affected by the action."[84] This is generally called the greatest happiness principle. Morally *good* is therefore what brings the biggest outcome for the largest number of people, which means what brings the "greatest sum total of utility."[85] Utilitarianism is similar "to what we know as *cost–benefit analysis*"[86] since to every action or person a utility

Think Outside the Box

As a business person, **cost–benefit analysis** and thus **utilitarianism** will sound familiar to you.

But reflect:

*   Are you only trying to maximize your company's profit?
*   (How) does your business calculate with people (employees, customers, and so forth)?
*   Are they only numbers to you or are they perceived as individuals?
*   How do you know if your decisions are good and for whom?

can be assigned. The one action with the biggest utility is the morally correct one. Now ask yourself: What would that mean for ResCoCo? In egoism you would just freely decide what is best for ResCoCo—probably in monetary terms. In utilitarianism you would need to figure out which decision brings a bigger outcome for the largest number of people. If you had to lay off 50 people in your premises but you could make sure that you would not infringe human rights of, say, 100 people: would you then ensure that the happiness in total is greater? You see, there is no right or wrong!

Now it is your turn. To get familiar with this thinking try the following: next time you make a decision, take five minutes and try to imagine *all* possible consequences, not only in terms of profits but also in terms of ecological and social impacts. You will probably realize fast that this is quite an impossible undertaking and thus is not practically realizable on a day-to-day basis.

2.2.4 Nonconsequentialist Ethics

Nonconsequentialist ethics approaches, as the expression already mentions, are not concerned with the consequences or outcomes of actions. Instead, they allocate inherent **rights** or **duties** to human beings. Within duty ethics, also called deontological ethics, ethical principles are justified without considering the consequences.[87] The *intention* is what is decisive.

To make *the rights of others* more tangible for you as the reader of this book, I now consider a globally recognized set that is linked to nonconsequentialism: **fundamental human rights**. The term human rights has been already mentioned several times up until now. I am aware of the fact that a modern ethics is not an applied ethics but should be discursive. Yet to put it into practice, I argue for taking into consideration the internationally recognized Universal

> ## Think Outside the Box
>
> Could you as a controller or a business student imagine that moral behavior based only on the good intention is equivalent in its importance to target setting when it comes to steering your company?
>
> What could be a controller's duties from a moral perspective?

Declaration of Human Rights announced by the United Nations[88] when talking about rights. By acknowledging the fundamental human rights, this book follows the so-called Ruggie framework. In his 2008 report to the Human Rights Council of the United Nations, Ruggie—in his function as special representative of the secretary-general on the issue of human rights—stresses the respect of *all* human rights "as the baseline responsibility of companies."[89] Hence, I want to display Article 1 of the Universal Declaration of Human Rights, which states the following:

> All human beings are born free and equal in dignity and rights. They are endowed with reason and conscience and should act toward one another in a spirit of brotherhood.[90]

This article is consistent with the unimpeachable freedom of all persons involved, which you found when I introduced the term morality.

In contrast to teleological ethics—which is asking how we *would like* to live—duty ethics raises the question how one *should* act.[91] If you are a nonethicist and you have not been introduced to ethical thinking in the past, it may seem difficult at first glance. One easy way to deal with deontological ethics is Kant's second maxim of his categorical imperative:

> Act in such a way as to treat humanity, whether in your own person or in that of anyone else, always as an end and never merely as a means.[92]

That so-called *human-end-formula* implies that it is by no means valid to make people a pure instrument in order to achieve other (but lower) objectives. Hence, it emphasizes that the instrumental Homo Oeconomicus is entirely opposite of Kant's moral principle[93] since the Homo Oeconomicus does not take into account the dignity of others. Moreover, Kant stresses that a human being as an end "doesn't have a mere relative value (a *price*) but has intrinsic value (i.e., dignity)."[94] Hence, the *value of any person is not calculable*. This should be a valid moral concept for every human being and thus should also be the argumentation why a company should engage in responsible behavior. At ResCoCo, a nonconsequentialist approach would mean the following: the good intention of the decision is what counts. The consequences—either layoffs or human rights infringements—would not be taken into account. However, if ResCoCo's controller applies Article 1 of the Universal Declaration of Human Rights, it will be clear that human rights infringe-

> ## Think Outside the Box
>
> - What do you think: Is it legitimate to calculate with human beings?
> - How do you personally justify the layoff of some employees in case a machine would be cheaper?
> - Have you ever applied this method in a private environment? Maybe counted the costs of a new car versus a good education of yourself and your family?

ments cannot be tolerated. Remember that all human beings are equal in dignity and rights! And how does it appear when taking Kant's *human-end-formula* into account? In this approach, it is reprehensible to count with human beings. Consequently, ResCoCo's controller must not compare internal staff with supplier's employees. You might argue now that this approach is an unsatisfactory basis for decision making. But think of the situation where you had to weigh people against a machine. Taking Kant seriously, it is never acceptable to only treat people as a means—also not as a means to profit maximization.

As you may now realize, it is not meaningful to see the different ethical approaches as opponents.[95] Crane and Matten therefore argue for a "pluralism"[96] of ethical theories in order to solve ethical dilemmas. Pluralism means that you should not take one sole ethics approach into account "as the only authority in questions of right and wrong."[97] Instead, it is suggested to take a "'prism' of (different) ethical theories"[98] instead of a "lens"[99] of one ethical approach. Considering ethics, which is basically a reflection effort, and its different theories will help you to develop a moral understanding in order to make legitimate decisions. Maybe there is no right or wrong, but most likely there are better or worse decisions.

Why Should an Organization Assume Responsibility?

Because every human being should always be treated as an end in itself and should never be seen as a mere instrument to be successful.

To conclude this chapter, it can be said that from an ethical perspective a company should assume responsibility since it consists of and deals with human beings. Human beings both have human dignity themselves and should regard the human dignity of others as a fundamental principle. Thus, responsibility must be grounded on moral considerations and not on profit maximization. Following an integrative economic ethics, it can be summarized that there are no ethically neutral spheres.

Real-Life Examples of Dealing With Responsibility Seriously

Economy for the Common Good—An Economic Model for the Future[100]

The aim of this initiative is to introduce another kind of economic behavior that is based on cooperation, fairness toward all stakeholders, and respect for the natural environment. The Economy for the Common Good initiative started in October 2010 and can already look back at an immense success. It is supported not only by NGOs, but also by politicians, individuals, and *companies.* This shows that there are certainly companies that are not content with today's economic behavior. Over 300 companies have already created a *Common Good Balance Sheet.* This tool is very valuable if you want to get an overview on your corporation's behavior in the realms of human dignity, cooperation and solidarity, ecological sustainability, social justice, and democratic co-determination and transparency. I can highly suggest taking some time and filling out the balance sheet. But before doing so, be aware of the fact that within the triple bottom line a balance sheet must not only contain financial figures. The balance sheet in the first step is a self-assessment that you are doing together with peer companies and maybe other interested persons. It includes a scoring model that allows assessing your corporate behavior. What is very interesting is the fact that you also get negative points when, for example, abusing human rights.

If you want to dig deeper, you find more detailed information on the following website:

www.gemeinwohl-oekonomie.org/en/

Alternative Bank Switzerland—Acting According to Ethical Principles[101]

The Alternative Bank Switzerland is a small bank acting according to ethical principles in Switzerland. Its aims are, among others, to act for the common good, for the human beings themselves and for the natural environment. The money of the bank's customers is exclusively invested in social and ecological projects in the real economy. The ethical principles of the bank are leading within the projects and thus lead to a conscious rejection of profit maximization. One may now critically argue that there are many companies that make statements like these. However, what are often empty words seems to be day-to-day reality at the Alternative Bank Switzerland. A high-transparency approach releases all loans publicly, indicating names, the amount of money, and the intended purpose. Moreover, every year, an external ethics control body examines the bank's operations and presents an ethical audit report.

This example shows that even or better: especially in the finance area, there are ways to change corporate behavior toward a more responsible one. Prerequisite, however, is the reflection of the actual way of doing business.

2.2.5 Some Points to Remember

In general, we can find two impetuses for CSR:

1. The so-called business case for CSR and
2. An ethical understanding

The business case understanding, on the one hand, asks how a company can reap benefit from a responsible behavior. This is not per se reprehensible. On the other hand, in an ethical understanding, "business ethics is the study of business situations, activities, and decisions where issues of (morally) right and wrong are addressed."[102] Integrative business ethics thinking perceives ethics as the inherent basis for every business action, instead of seeing it as a boundary. It critically reflects the actual way of doing business. Hence, there are no ethically neutral spheres.

Kant's *human-end-formula* implies that it is by no means valid to make people a pure instrument in order to achieve other (but lower) objectives. It is not legitimate to calculate with human beings. A company should assume responsibility since it consists of and deals with human beings. Responsibility, therefore, must be grounded on morality and not on profit maximization.

2.3   Concretizing Responsibility

Within this chapter, I show (a) *which* responsibilities a company could have and (b) for *whom* a company may assume responsibilities. Let us start with which responsibilities may be assumed.

2.3.1   Which Responsibilities Does an Organization Have?

Once we have accepted and understood "that every right implies a responsibility; every opportunity an obligation; every possession, a duty"[103] we may ask *which* responsibility we or our organization could have. Earlier it was stated that the social responsibility of corporations consists of four categories: (1) economic, (2) legal, (3) ethical, and (4) discretionary expectations, which "society has of organizations at a given point of time"[104] and which exist simultaneously. Let us examine them.

1. Carroll claims that the first responsibility of a corporation is an **economic** one.[105] However, this responsibility—Carroll calls it the "bedrock foundation for business"[106]—does not mean pure profit maximization. Rather it means "to produce goods and services that society wants and sell them at a profit."[107] The *profit* notion indicates that stockholders are not neglected and that we do not talk about pure philanthropy at this stage. In some countries, the management board

has a legal obligation toward shareholders. However, what is an appropriate profit is not easy to define and depends on context-specific factors. Carroll points to the fact that it depends on the country that a corporation is conducting business in, but that profit in general is the basis that a corporation needs in order to survive.[108] The economic responsibility is also to be seen in providing employees a safe job (think about ResCoCo) and pay them in a fair manner.[109] This shows that other stakeholders as well as the stockholders are considered.

2. Considering the **legal** aspects of the total social responsibilities, there are numerous laws and legal systems within different countries.[110] The German Commercial Code, for example, compels large capital companies to integrate nonfinancial key performance indicators such as environmental and employee topics into their statement of affairs.[111] In spite of the fact that there are different national laws, we could define the legal responsibilities as the "ground rules"[112] corporations have to comply with within a special country.

3. The third category, according to Carroll, is to be seen in the **ethical** responsibilities.[113] Although he confesses that it is difficult to define them properly, they are described as the expectation "society has . . . of business over and above legal requirements."[114] Others call them the actions that are "right, just, and fair"[115] but that are not imposed by laws. At this point, I would like to stress the link to the CSR and sustainability definition drawn up earlier. There, you have seen that CSR is conducted on a voluntary basis, over and above legal requirements. Carroll, however, also subsumes the economic, the legal, and the discretionary responsibilities under a corporation's social responsibility.[116] Hence you realize now that it is difficult to define exactly what responsibilities a company should assume.

4. Considering the **discretionary** responsibilities, in his 1979 paper, Carroll himself is unsure if these are real responsibilities. Rather, these are voluntary actions.[117] However, more recently, he states that society often sees philanthropy as an expected—even though not clear-cut—business behavior.[118]

Distinguishing among economic, legal, ethical, and discretionary responsibilities may a) not be easy and would b) violate the fact that ethics should be the fundamental principle of all economic behavior. Carroll admits that the four responsibilities, which he claims, exist simultaneously and are not mutually exclusive.[119] Yet, in my viewpoint, the impression could be created that the economic factors are the most important ones. To answer *what* responsibilities should be considered more concretely for the purpose of establishing a responsible controlling framework, I do not set Carroll's four stages as the basis. As an alternative, the following approach is suggested:

A corporation should assume all **responsibilities** that are based on **legitimate claims**. Precisely this means and requires

- taking into account *economic, ecological, and social* considerations (the effects on the **triple bottom line** have to be considered when conducting business);
- always taking **morality** (meaning the mutual recognition of the dignity of all human beings) into consideration as the **unconditional foundation** for every decision and behavior.

What is not yet clearly defined is the *scope* and the *boundary* of social responsibilities. The financial consolidation boundary as normally valid for controlling does not necessarily represent the boundary for social responsibilities ascribed to corporations.[120] Companies should also consider responsibilities that may not directly lie in their sphere of financial influence. The next section looks at the question for whom a corporation is responsible.

Think Outside the Box

- Make a list:
  What do you think are your responsibilities in every column of the triple bottom line (economic, ecological, and social factors)? Where do you assume negative consequences of your actions?
- Have you assumed these responsibilities in the past? If not, what would you need to change?
- Have you always taken into account the human dignity of your stakeholders when you made decisions in the past?

2.3.2 For Whom Is an Organization Responsible?—Considering Stakeholders

When having stated that morality should be the unconditional foundation on which responsibility ought to be grounded, we have unconsciously admitted that responsibility is assumed toward human beings. The question at this point is toward *which* human beings a company takes over responsibilities and if and where there are boundaries of responsibilities. If we reject Friedman's view that the only responsibility of corporate executives is "to make as much money for their stockholders as possible,"[121] we may question who else is to be taken into account. That is, who else may have a stake in the corporation? Freeman states that a "stakeholder in an organization is . . . any group or individual who can affect or is affected by the achievement of the organization's objectives."[122] To make it more tangible for practical application, one may argue on this basis that a stakeholder "is harmed by, or benefits from, the corporation; *or* (is somebody) whose rights can be violated, or have to be respected, by the corporation."[123] This argumentation is based on Evan and Freeman's observation, who talk about the use of two principles:

1. The one of a corporation's *effects* (harm or benefits) on others and their responsibility for their actions, and
2. The (respected or violated) *rights*, meaning that it is imperative to not infringe others' rights.[124]

This is a broad basis for the definition of stakeholders. The ones who can be harmed, for example, may be thousands of kilometers away and may not be recognized as being affected. Mitchell, Agle, and Wood point to the fact that Freeman's definition does not clarify for whom a corporation *should* or actually *does* assume responsibility.[125] They raise two questions:

1. Who are the stakeholders of the firm?[126] and
2. To whom (or what) do managers (actually) pay attention?[127]

According to the authors, the former question suggests for a "*normative theory of stakeholder identification.*"[128] That is, it asks why specific groups or individuals *should* be acknowledged as stakeholders. The second question takes as a basis a *"descriptive theory of stakeholder salience,"*[129] which demonstrates to whom a corporation actually *does* ascribe importance to in reality. Within today's business life, obviously stakeholder power is the prevailing factor with regard to the identification of stakeholders. Thielemann and Wettstein criticize that the ones who have much power when it comes to a corporation's profit making are seen as the company's key stakeholders.[130] Key stakeholders are unfortunately seen as the ones "who are relevant or significant *for the company's bottom line*"[131]— but not necessarily for the ecological and social dimension of the *triple* bottom line. Thus, it is not surprising that a survey about sustainability among 500 German medium-sized companies revealed that employees and customers are the most important factors, even when it comes to sustainability.[132] As drivers for sustainable behavior, the respondents mentioned the increase in customer trust and customer loyalty as the most important ones, followed by protection of the company, employee loyalty, increase in sales, recruiting of new employees, and an increase in good reputation.[133] Schaltegger, Windolph, and Harms, in another survey, found out that media and the public are rated highest by corporations when asked about who drives them in a sustainable direction. Moreover, nongovernmental organizations (NGOs) are mentioned even before the customers.[134] This is a big difference to the first mentioned survey conducted by Englisch et al., who see the customer at the first place. Consequently, there is no unambiguous idea about who *are* the corporation's most important stakeholders.

Unfortunately, the surveys did not ask if moral reasons could be a stimulus for managers in order to engage in a responsible behavior. Rather, what is listed earlier creates the impression that companies are only following an instrumentalist view—even when it comes to responsibility itself. However, in line with the objective of bringing responsibility thinking into corporations, stakeholder management that asks who *should* be taken into consideration can be identified as the most legitimate approach. Thielemann and Wettstein argue that "the argumentatively strongest stakeholders are not necessarily the most 'relevant' ones for the company."[135] In accordance with Mitchell, Agle, and Wood they differentiate two stakeholder approaches: (a) "normative-ethical understanding"[136] (according to Freeman, that means the stakeholder *is affected*

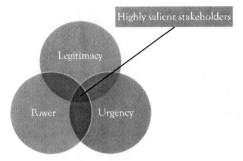

Figure 2.2 Stakeholder classification

Source: Mitchell, Agle, and Wood, "Toward a Theory of Stakeholder Identification and Salience: Defining the Principle of Who and What Really Counts," p. 872. © 1997, Vol. 22, No. 4, 853–886. Reprinted with permission from Academy of Management Review.

by the company and should therefore be considered) and (b) an approach in which stakeholders "are seen simply as constraints to profit-maximization."[137] This relates to Freeman's expression that the company *can affect* the stakeholders. Considering power as the most important factor when it comes to the identification and classification of stakeholders, it is to be seen as an "ethics withouth morals . . . (and therefore) an *ethics of the right of the powerful*."[138] Further, I would like to follow a normative approach when raising the question which stakeholders *ought to* be taken into account. This approach is based on three dimensions: power, legitimacy, and urgency (Figure 2.2).[139] Stakeholders who only have power, urgent claims, *or* legitimate arguments are seen as latent. If they belong to two of the three dimensions they are expectant. Only if they can claim all three aspects they are "highly salient stakeholders."[140] Still, it is to admit that salience is a moving condition because power, urgency, and legitimacy can change over time.[141] Some criticize this approach, since it neglects legitimacy as the ultimately decisive "criterion for the recognition of claims."[142] At this point, Kant comes into play again, when the second maxim of the categorical imperative is reformulated by Thielemann and Wettstein as follows: "what counts is not power, but good reasons."[143] What is to be avoided is the "Strategic Stakeholder Synthesis,"[144] where stakeholders without power might simply be neglected.

To conclude this section, Ulrich's integrative economic ethics approach should be considered. As Thielemann and Wettstein do, he also states that the ultimately decisive criterion of who counts is to be seen

Think Outside the Box

- Who *has been* regarded as a stakeholder in the past?
- Who *should be* regarded as a stakeholder if you want to take into account the fact that your actions should not infringe upon the dignity of every human being?
- Have you answered questions one and two same or different?

in the legitimacy of the claims, which means that it is important who should be able to raise legitimate claims, and not who really has the power to do so.[145] It does not mean that a corporation is not allowed to make profits. After all, these profits may be used to pay employees or to settle invoices of your suppliers. But profit needs to be justified on the basis of legitimate grounds. Ulrich confesses that there may be problems of reasonableness when it comes to stakeholder claims. However, both responsibility toward stakeholders and the question of reasonableness must be considered within a discourse.[146]

Hence, within this book, as stakeholders I understand every group or individual who has legitimate claims regarding the behavior of our corporation. This means I take into account all people involved who have rights—rights not only in terms of legal contracts but first and foremost in the light of not being infringed upon their human dignity. Remembering the Brundtland Report, it comes to our mind that there is also *inter*generational responsibility. Therefore, I would like to introduce another dimension, which should be called "future generations." Subsequently, I refer to the following definition of stakeholders when answering for whom responsibility should be assumed:

A stakeholder is every group or individual—living today or in the future—who *has* legitimate claims, regardless of whether the stakeholder has the power to really make the claim or not. The basic principle in considering stakeholders thereby must be seen in humans' **morality** and thus in the **unimpeachable human dignity**.

In the light of this definition, ResCoCo should identify its stakeholders. Undoubtedly, supplier's employees need to be taken into account as well—although they may not have the power to influence ResCoCo's business behavior.

2.3.3   Some Points to Remember

A corporation should **assume all responsibilities** that are **based on legitimate claims**. Precisely, it means (a) taking into account the **effects on the triple bottom line** when conducting business and (b) always taking the **human dignity** into consideration as the unconditional foundation for every decision and behavior.

Moreover, there are two basic questions when it comes to stakeholders:

1. Who **should be** the stakeholders of a company because they have **legitimate claims?**
2. Who **is really paid attention** to because they have much **power?**

In reality, question two is the prevalent one.

I understand a stakeholder as every group or individual—living today or in the future—who has legitimate claims, regardless of whether the stakeholder has the power to really make the claim or not. The basic principle in considering stakeholders thereby must be seen in humans' morality and thus in the unimpeachable human dignity.

Following the careful examination of the theoretical background of responsibility, sustainabilty, and ethics, the next chapter will have a close look at *controlling.*

CHAPTER 3

Management Accounting and Controlling: A Basic Introduction

"Not everything that can be counted counts and not everything that counts can be counted."[1]

—Albert Einstein

This book deals with the topic of responsible controlling. So far, we have elaborated on the first part of this word composition. Yet, the term *controlling* has not been regarded in detail. Therefore, in order to synthesize both expressions later on, we now consider controlling. For the purpose of thorough understanding, I first elaborate what is to be understood by controlling. I do so by considering different views on controlling from contemporary literature. Moreover, you will get to know the prevalent basic controlling tasks before analyzing the current trends in controlling when it comes to environmental and social topics (Chapter 4).

3.1 Controlling in an Organizational Context—Setting the Stage

3.1.1 Controlling—A Basic Introduction

The term controlling can be derived from different languages. The Middle English word *counter-roll* and the French notion *contre-rôle* mean that the actual asset base is checked against the nominal state by using a list. *Compte*—a French expression—and *conto*, which is Italian, mean *account*. Hence, the initial *comptrolling* stands for the examination of accounts.[2] This shows that controlling apparently deals with financial topics.

However, beyond the umbrella term finance, it is not totally clear what exactly is the content of controlling. More than 40 years ago, Harvard Business School professor Robert Anthony mentions that "in practice, people with the title controller have functions that are, at one extreme little more than bookkeeping, at the other extreme, de facto general management."[3] This quote indicates that, back then, there was no clear-cut definition of controlling. This is still true today, even though there are some fundamental agreements within the prevailing literature. These common grounds are emphasized in the following text.

First, controlling must neither be confused with (a) internal accounting, nor with (b) external accounting. The latter, which is also called financial reporting, deals with balance sheets and with profit and loss accounts. Yet, according to Eschenbach and Siller, both internal and external accounting are to be seen as fundamental data sources for controlling.[4] Figure 3.1 gives a first impression that accounting and controlling are related, both are concerned with financial topics, but are not the same.

Accounting, especially the external accounting, which is based on legislation, puts its focus on the accuracy of the figures used. Controlling, by contrast, directs its attention to (not only financial) values and strategies. Figures are also of high interest, but may not be as exact as

	External accounting	Internal accounting	Controlling
Context	Focus on accurate figures	Focus on accurate figures	Focus on values, strategies, and figures
Time	Past	Past / future	Future
Culture	Provision of numbers	Provision of numbers	Provision and interpretation of numbers
Priority	Accuracy first, actuality second	Accuracy first, actuality second	Actuality first, accuracy second → derivation of measures
Output and recipients	Annual financial statement; for internal and external stakeholders	Calculations, income statements per period; for internal stakeholders	Reports, proposals regarding measures, planning system; for internal stakeholders

Figure 3.1 Accounting versus controlling

Source: Eschenbach and Siller (2009), p. 88. © 2009, Schäffer-Poeschel. Reprinted with permission from Schäffer-Poeschel.

in accounting. With regard to the time frame, external accounting uses the rearview mirror, in the sense that figures that were gathered in the past are being reported. On the contrary, controlling is future oriented. Numbers, which are in parts taken from accounting, are not only provided but also interpreted with the objective of deriving measures for the future. In controlling, timeliness and actuality are more important than the accuracy of the figures. Einstein's expression that "not everything that can be counted counts and not everything that counts can be counted"[5] may be a good slogan for controlling as well, because controlling creates reports, makes proposals, and provides planning systems for internal stakeholders of the corporation, like the owners, management, and employees. In contrast, external accounting releases the annual financial statement for both internal and external stakeholders and thus must be more accurate.[6]

Within the English speaking literature, the term management accounting is more common than the term controlling. According to the Institute of Management Accountants

> Management accounting is a profession that involves partnering in management decision making, devising planning and performance management systems, and providing expertise in financial reporting and control to assist management in the formulation and implementation of an organization's strategy.[7]

Becker, analyzing the differences between the European controlling and the American management accounting approaches, claims that **controlling** and **management accounting** can be perceived as being **equivalent** even though varying definitions can be found in the literature.[8]

We observe that accounting and controlling have a commonality: they both deal with figures. In addition, I have shown the basic differences of accounting and controlling. Yet, it is still unclear what exactly is to be understood by controlling. Ziegenbein pictures controlling as

> The selection and application of methods . . . and information for planning and monitoring processes . . ., as well as the cross-functional coordination . . . of these processes.[9]

He sees coordination as the outer frame, while information and methods are the inner frame of reference in order to perform planning and monitoring.

Wöhe and Döring define controlling as

> The sum of all measures . . ., which serve to coordinate the areas of management (which are) planning, monitoring, organization, personnel management and information, in a way which ensures that the corporate objectives can be accomplished in the optimum manner.[10]

Hence, coordination is one of the central aspects of controlling. Moreover, planning, monitoring, and information can be found in both aforementioned definitions. Weber and Schäffer introduce a term that is closely linked to the comprehension of today's controlling: rationality.[11] In their understanding, rationality is to be thought as instrumental or purposive rationality. Accordingly, resources need to be used efficiently in order to achieve given purposes or ends.[12] Since it is the target of this book to base controlling on an ethical basis, it is to ask what Weber and Schäffer understand as given ends. When establishing a responsible controlling framework below, I return to rationality again.

Horváth comprehends controlling as a subsystem that supports management by coordinating, planning, and monitoring and by providing information with respect to targets.[13] Weissmann argues that controlling as a service function for objective decision making helps to steer a company by using targets.[14] Targets have to be implemented, monitored, and, if necessary, actions have to be taken in order to reach these targets. In addition, he argues, following Gutenberg,[15] that management (not controlling) uses the instruments of planning, organization, and monitoring.[16] Remembering Ziegenbein's definition of controlling, which is about planning and monitoring processes, we now realize that the terms of controlling and management are not separated accurately, even within today's prevailing literature.

To arrive at a better understanding of what is controlling, I take a closer look at controllers and managers as persons. The International Group of Controlling mentions that "as partners of management controllers make a significant contribution to the sustainable success of the organization."[17] The group's controller mission statement declares that a controller should

- "design and accompany the management process of defining goals, planning and management control so that every decision maker can act in accordance with agreed objectives;
- . . . . ensure the conscious preoccupation with the future and thus make it possible to take advantage of opportunities and manage risks;
- . . . . integrate an organization's goals and plans into a cohesive whole;
- . . . . develop and maintain all management control systems. They ensure the quality of data and provide decision-relevant information;
- . . . . (be) the economic conscience and thus committed to the good of an organization as a whole."[18]

In accordance with that, the International Controllers Association[19] illustrates the depicted separation (or cooperation) of managers and controllers.[20]

As can be seen in Figure 3.2 the International Controllers Association understands controlling as the interaction of managers and controllers. Managers, on the one hand, bear responsibility for the business results

Figure 3.2 Controlling as cooperation of managers and controllers

and for finance matters, as well as for the corporation's processes and strategy, that should lead to a successfully run business. Controllers, on the other hand, need to bring transparency into the (results of the) managers' tasks.[21] This is not done by mere supervision or monitoring. Instead, controllers ensure that all people involved can monitor themselves by making use of the established controlling systems. Moreover, controllers have the "legitimation to unsolicited advice"[22] toward the management board. To allow transparency, the controller is in charge of establishing the process of controlling by using adequate tools and methods.[23] *Controlling as a process is the result of the interaction between managers and controllers.* It needs to be noted that controlling can only proceed if there is awareness for controlling as a steering and control system of the corporation.[24] The Austrian Controlling Institute[25] explains that controlling can be seen as a mindset that ought to be applied by all executives. Furthermore, it says that controlling is to be understood as a philosophy of management and leadership that all executives (should) follow.[26]

It is to highlight that the definition as *mindset* is distinct from the other explanations. However, they are not mutually exclusive. In the latter, functional understanding, controlling must be a philosophy of management, which means it must be accepted and executed by all people involved.[27] Yet, within this book, we will follow an institutional view of controlling in contrast to the mere functional perspective. I see controlling as an institution, which means at least as one individual person or even as a department that establishes the controlling process. In the functional view, controlling would be executed by the management itself what implies the risk of overemphasized individual or divisional interests. The aforementioned self-control may not work in every situation. With controlling as an institution, it can be ensured that the overall corporate interests are taken into account.[28] Whether controlling is conceptualized as staff unit or as a separate department within the line organization is not relevant for the definition of controlling tasks.

Until now it has been shown that controlling arises from the cooperation of controllers and managers. According to these definitions, different attributes are ascribed to controlling. I use the aforementioned common features in order to sum up controlling in the purpose of this book as follows.

3.1.2 Some Points to Remember

Controlling

- is an organizational subsystem that **supports management** to reach the agreed targets by establishing, moderating, and (cross-functionally) **coordinating** adequate controlling systems and a controlling process;
- does not only have a service function but also has the **responsibility** for **transparency**, which means controlling has a co-responsibility for corporate success;
- **provides** timely and actual monetary and nonmonetary **information** in order to ensure **(instrumental) rationality** and thus;
- is highly involved in **objective decision making** processes;
- uses methods of **planning** and **monitoring**;
- perceives **internal stakeholders**, above all the management, as recipients;
- is **communication** and is dependent on **interaction**; and
- is conceptualized as a separated **institution** within the corporation.

Having now made a basic summarizing definition, the next section further examines controlling by presenting several areas. Moreover, the controlling cycle and the controlling process model are elaborated before the notion of key performance indicators (KPIs) are introduced.

3.2 Concretizing Controlling

3.2.1 Established Controlling Areas

In the prevailing literature, controlling is mostly separated into **strategic controlling** and **operational controlling**. Both of them basically have the same task, which is to be seen in management support.[29] The first one uses the aforementioned methods such as coordination, planning, and monitoring as a service for strategic corporate management, while the latter utilizes them in relation to the operational management.[30]

	Strategic controlling	Operational controlling
Controlling-support for...	Strategic objectives	Operational objectives
Target dimension	Securing the corporation's existence	Profit
Basic terms	Chances & risks; strengths & weaknesses	Revenues & expenses; planned-actual-comparisons
Parameters / key indicators	Success potentials	Profitability
Type of information	Qualitative and quantitative	Quantitative
Time	Remote future	Present & near future
Type of activities	Innovative	Routine; well structured
Approach	Doing the right things	Doing the things right
Role of controlling	Change agent, advisor, driver & brakesman	Analyst, advisor, driver & brakesman
Tool	Telescope	Microscope

Figure 3.3 Strategic and operational controlling

Source: Eschenbach and Siller (2009), Preißler (2007), Buchholz (2009), and Baum, Coenenberg, and Günther (2007). © 2009, Schäffer-Poeschel. Adapted and reprinted with permission from Schäffer-Poeschel.

However, in practice, strategic and operational controlling are usually not separated.[31] Yet, there are some major differences that are presented in Figure 3.3.

Think Outside the Box

If you are a controller, are you acting as a change agent? Are you bringing new ideas into the company and realizing what is going on outside the company?

If you are a manager, are you perceiving your controller as a change agent or rather as a bean counter? For making controlling responsible, you better have the first one!

One of the most important differences between strategic and operational controlling is to be seen in the target dimension. Strategic controlling is engaged in securing the corporation's long-term existence.[32] To do so, chances and risks are considered and strengths and weaknesses are evaluated[33] with the aim of identifying and creating success potentials for the existence of the corporation. Success potentials are to be created in the long term. As a success potential, for example, product development and the development of a strong market position can be named.[34] On this basis, the corporation can achieve profits and durable success.[35] From the viewpoint of operational controlling, medium-term profit is of more importance.[36] Therefore, it takes into account revenues and expenses[37] and uses planned–actual comparisons[38] to take corrective measures, if necessary. Both, operational and strategic controlling deal with quantitative information. But strategic controlling also highly uses qualitative information.[39] Buchholz states that strategic controlling is about *doing the right things*, while operational controlling is concerned with *doing the things right*.[40] This is what Drucker calls effectiveness and efficiency, respectively.[41] Strategic controlling must be innovative and should not only be advisory for management but should also be a change agent in order to ensure the company's long-term existence.[42] Being a *change agent* seems to go beyond the previously elaborated information provider. Recalling that it is the aim to make controlling responsible and make it a driver toward sustainability, the notion change agent will come into play again later.

In addition to the theoretical distinction of strategic and operational controlling, in practice, different hyphenated controlling areas can be found. Schäffer and Weber distinguish 12 different (hyphenated) controlling types: purchasing-controlling, research and development-controlling, production-controlling, marketing and sales-controlling, logistics and supply chain-controlling, personnel-controlling, finance-controlling, information technology-controlling, environmental-controlling, project-controlling, equity-controlling, and cooperation-controlling.[43] Each of them executes the controlling tasks shown earlier within a single corporate realm.

So far, we have had an overview in which different areas and characteristics controlling is performed. **Controlling is about decision making.** Decisions are made in every function of a corporation—controlling correlates to that. Therefore, I refrain from further discussing every controlling function and area in detail. With respect to the objective of this book, I will instead have a look at the controlling cycle and at KPIs for decision making, regardless of whether production, purchasing, or finance is involved.

3.2.2 Controlling Cycle and Process Model

In the previous sections, we have figured out that controlling has to do with planning and monitoring. When having a look at the prevailing literature on controlling, it is evident that these two notions are part of a cycle. Tschandl, for instance, shows a six-step *controlling cycle*.[44] Eschenbach and Siller mention the notions of plan-do-check-act (PDCA)[45] as a cybernetic loop that needs to be supported by controlling when talking about corporate management. They refer to the so-called PDCA cycle, which is particularly known in quality management and which is used as a process for problem solving and a method for process improvement.[46] When managing processes, four steps should be considered.

First, the issue has to be identified and a **plan** for dealing with the issue has to be set up based on data that is important for the process. Second, the plan is executed (**do**). Afterward, it is to check if the desired results were achieved (**check**)—again on basis of relevant data, which needs to be gathered and analyzed. As a fourth step (**act**), the next measures are identified and the loop is started again if necessary.[47]

The PDCA cycle is also used for the management and control process within organizations. Controlling is involved in different steps of the PDCA cycle. It is included in planning (first step)—by agreeing on targets between management and controlling—as well as in checking or monitoring the results of the measures (third step) and in acting toward the target by initiating corrective measures (fourth step).[48] Related to corrective measures, one can differentiate between (a) "feedback" and (b) "feedforward."[49] Feedback implies that corrective measures of the intended execution are made in order to achieve the agreed targets. Feedforward means changing the target or plan due to altered preconditions in the corporation's environment. These preconditions lead to the circumstance that it is not sufficient if controlling—understood as navigating or steering—only regards internal factors. Instead, it must be recognized that the intended results may be altered and influenced by external conditions, without the deliberate involvement of controlling.[50]

The International Group of Controlling focuses on another approach called controlling process model.[51] The model defines main processes in controlling, which are shown in Figure 3.4. Each of them has more

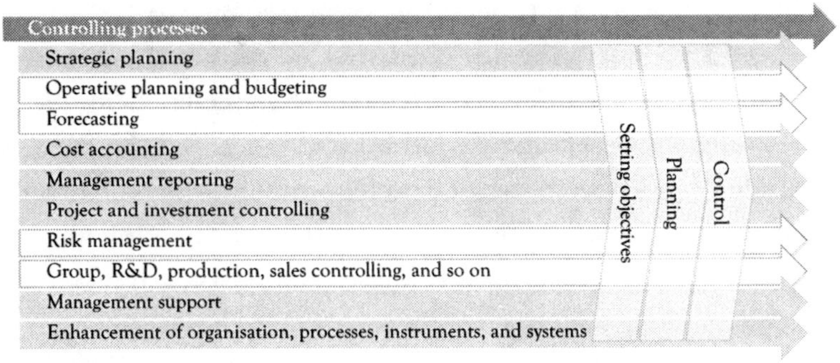

Figure 3.4 Controlling process model

Source: From International Group of Controlling (2012). Reprinted with permission by courtesy of Haufe Verlag.

detailed subprocesses. Setting objectives, planning, and control are tasks applied within all processes. Consequently, they lie across all sections.[52]

For our purposes I propose a merger of the PDCA cycle and the controlling process model, which are both very valuable approaches especially when it comes to the question of developing a responsible controlling framework itself. Instead of regarding setting objectives, planning, and control as a sequence of horizontal linear arrows that stop with the *control* part, it is the PDCA cycle that should lie across all the controlling main processes.

The main processes of the controlling process model cannot be regarded as mutually exclusive. Yet, the process model gives you a good overview and may allow to define where we can start to make controlling more responsible (shown in light gray color in Figure 3.4). But what is relevant with respect to sustainability, responsibility, and ethics? Within this book, we will especially deal with the process of *enhancement of organisation, processes, instruments and systems* when it comes to the elaboration of a responsible controlling framework. Subprocesses within this section are the continuous development of controlling itself as well as disseminating knowledge regarding new instruments. Also of interest for our purposes could be the *strategic planning* section, which includes the following: examining vision, mission, values, and the underlying business model. Moreover, the International Group of Controlling mentions that the relevant stakeholders should be included in drawing up the strategy.

In addition, targets have to be agreed on, measures should be decided, and the relevant KPIs must be implemented. Also *cost accounting* and *management reporting* may have relevance in terms of responsibility. With respect to *project and investment controlling*, this main process includes the decision making process for projects. Controlling must provide tools in order to facilitate the decision making process for management. This aspect is mentioned again in the *management support* process where it is said that the decision making processes must be accompanied by controlling.[53]

What is relevant for all processes within the model are KPIs. They come into play when controlling is supporting management in terms of making strategies and decisions. In the following, it is clarified what is to be understood by KPIs and how KPIs, provided by controlling, contribute to an objective managerial decision making.

3.2.3   KPIs for Decision Making

Key Performance Indicators try to reduce complexity in order to make better informed decisions.

KPIs are to be understood as figures that explain managerial issues and developments in a compact manner. For controlling, they are an important tool[54] whose aim is to reduce the corporation's complexity.[55] According to Gladen, quantitative information is more appropriate than qualitative information in order to give management a good overview.[56] However, with regard to choosing appropriate KPIs, instead of the possibility of comfortably measuring them, nowadays rather the relevance for corporation's success is taken into account.[57] Irrespective of whether quantitative or qualitative, KPIs help to provide timely and actual monetary and nonmonetary information to management in order to ensure rationality in decision making. Traditionally, financial KPIs are seen as the most important.[58] Nevertheless, a well-balanced set of monetary and nonmonetary KPIs is needed. KPIs are necessary not only in terms of the information provision, but also in terms of analyzing and monitoring function of controlling[59] as well as to target setting and convenient communication.[60] In the sense of *key* performance indicators, it is important to not monitor all available figures but to only take into account the ones that play an important role for managing a corporation.[61]

Examining the nature of KPIs, they can be differentiated in (a) absolute and (b) relative ones.[62] Absolute KPIs are cardinal numbers like the sum of expenditures. Relative KPIs show a ratio of different figures and hence are also called *ratios*. These are further distinguished in three subcategories: (1) quotas, (2) reference numbers, and (3) index numbers. Quotas set a partial mass in relation to a total mass. This is the case if, for example, total sales is split into sales by different customers.[63] Reference numbers set two distinct figures in relation to each other, such as sales per employee.[64] Index numbers show the variance of equal figures over a period of time. This is, for example, to be seen in the sales of the previous year, which is the base number, in relation to the sales of the actual year.[65] The difference between the base number and the actual figure is expressed by the index number.

KPIs involve the risk of misinterpretations if only one KPI is regarded.[66] To avoid this, a set of KPIs should be taken into account. If several KPIs are put into an appropriate relationship against each other, a so-called KPI system is established.[67]

KPIs and KPI systems help management and controlling to better understand the corporation's situation and to make well-informed objective decisions. They are very valuable in the decision making process of

Put It to Practice

One of the best-known and easiest KPI systems probably is the DuPont scheme, which is also called return-on-investment (ROI) tree. The system was developed by E.I. DuPont de Nemours and Company and has been used since 1919. It easily explains how the return on investment is dependent both on capital turnover and return on sales and on all factors that affect these two. Its easiness is its advantage.[68] As a disadvantage I would like to name the short-term orientation. Long-term potentials are neglected. Moreover, from a sustainability perspective, it is to question if it is enough to only look at financial figures.

distinct situations, since they reduce much complexity and allow focusing on the relevant issues. To emphasize the importance of KPIs, one could cite Kaplan and Norton, who mention that "if you can't measure it, you can't manage it."[69] Drucker mentions in this sense that

> The measurement (that means the indicator, which is) used determines to what one pays attention. It makes things visible and tangible. The things included in the measurement become relevant; the things omitted are out of sight and out of mind.[70]

However, we figure out later if it is sufficient to have (only) adequately measurable KPIs in order to make decisions with respect to *responsibility*.

Up to this point, within this chapter, it has been clarified what is to be understood by controlling. Moreover, I have shown the areas in which controlling is present—strategic and operational controlling. Furthermore, the controlling cycle and the process model have been introduced, as well as the character of KPIs. With this basic understanding of established controlling, subsequently, current trends of controlling related to sustainability will be considered.

3.2.4   Some Points to Remember

- In theory, controlling is divided into (1) strategic and (2) operational controlling. The first is seeking to ensure the corporation's long-term existence. The second focuses on short-term profit making.
- Putting the plan-do-check-act cycle (controlling cycle) and the controlling process model together will help us to establish a responsible controlling framework.
- Absolute and relative KPIs try to reduce complexity and thus help to make more objective decisions.

CHAPTER 4

Current Controlling Trends Toward Sustainability and Responsibility

"After 36 years, 167 studies, and 16 reviews of the relationship between CSR and financial performance, the answer to the debate about whether CSR is profitable is unambiguously clear: "It depends.""[1]
—Raghubir et al.

It is traditionally one of the main tasks of controlling to support management in order to make decisions that contribute to the strategic and operational achievement of the corporate goals—which are mostly of the financial type.[2] With respect to sustainability, controlling must extend its focus onto ecological and social factors as well. In that sense, it is important to *integrate social and environmental topics into the existing controlling functions*, instead of creating a separated controlling view.[3] Yet, as mentioned earlier, to date, controlling is hardly involved when it comes to sustainability. That is a deficit.[4] Rational decisions can only be made on the basis of information like it is currently provided by controlling when it comes to financial matters. Now, information in terms of sustainability is needed.[5] In addition to the information function by quantifying sustainable aspects, Reichmann and Kißler see it as a controlling task to support management by *making use of controlling's methodological competence.*[6] The quality of information is the "bottleneck"[7] in sustainability management.

Taking into account controlling's support function for decision making, some state that management only needs and wants information about these facts that contribute to the target achievement. Controlling must measure these indicators in an objective way.[8] With respect to the intention of this book, I can agree on the fact that the triple bottom line must be taken into consideration in an integrative manner. Schalteg-ger, Windolph, and Harms add that information regarding sustainability must be integrated into existing information systems[9] instead of creat-ing a new system for sustainable measures itself. However, in responsi-ble controlling, it is to ask if it is sufficient to only consider these facts that contribute (positively) to the target achievement. This question is answered later. Now, two controlling realms associated with sustainability are examined. Later, information tools and two concepts with respect to the topic are elaborated.

4.1   Green Controlling

Within the European literature, the notion *green controlling*—coined by the International Controllers Association[10]—is more and more common. The term green in this context indicates that environmental factors are taken into consideration. In their edited book, Tschandl and Posch dis-cuss integrated environmental controlling.[11] More concretely, they stress the necessity to integrate environmental factors into conventional corpo-rate target systems and the relevance of having high-quality data.[12] Given the fact that Horváth, Isensee, and Michel discuss the notion of green controlling within the same book,[13] we will use green controlling and environmental controlling as synonyms.

Green Controlling Prize[14]

Since 2011, the Péter Horváth Foundation and the International Con-trollers Association award the Green Controlling Prize every year. They look for the most innovative and most effective green controlling solu-tions that help to steer ecological strategies, projects, and measures. With that they want to promote the green challenge of controllers and controlling departments.

In the last years, laureates have been, for example:

- Deutsche Post DHL for its "Carbon Accounting and Controlling"

(Continued)

- Hansgrohe SE for its program "Green Controlling—Green Profit—Green Future"
- Airport Stuttgart for its "fairport Controlling"
- Volkswagen AG for its environmental controlling in the context of "Think Blue. Factory."

Having a look into the journal *Controlling*, which issued a special edition *Green Controlling*, one can find the terms eco controlling,[15] environmental accounting systems,[16] and carbon footprint,[17] as well as a target costing approach that takes into account *green* factors.[18] The initiator of this green controlling movement is the International Controllers Association together with Horváth. The association issued a theoretical paper on green controlling and commissioned a study with respect to green controlling approaches. The study reveals that most of the respondents associate increasing energy efficiency, the reduction of greenhouse gas emissions, and the prevention of hazardous wastes with the term *green*.[19] Moreover, the study shows that the necessity for considering green aspects in controlling highly depends on the strategy that the company follows. Four different strategy types, in relation to which green controlling is conducted, are displayed in Figure 4.1.

Strategy **type 1** indicates that the corporation has a holistic green strategy, meaning that environmental aspects are relevant throughout the entire company—regarding its products and processes and including the supply chain. **Type 2** corporations focus mainly on green products and services and thus are market oriented. The observant strategy (**type 3**)

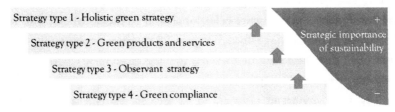

Figure 4.1 Green corporate strategy types influencing the type of green controlling

Source: Adapted and reprinted with permission from Internationaler Controller Verein, 2011, p. 11.

Think Outside the Box

In the quest for making a corporation more responsible holistically, is it acceptable to only take sustainable factors into account if they have a strategic corporate importance?

Or should a controller be a change agent and point out to material sustainability aspects that maybe have not been recognized yet by the board?

reveals that the corporation sees little strategic importance of environmental factors in the present. Strategy **type 4**—green compliance—means that the corporation is only willing to comply with or to slightly surpass existing ecological standards.[20] According to the International Controllers Association, it is not reprehensible that controlling instruments are only as elaborated as is the strategy of the company. If there is no strategic necessity to take environmental factors into consideration, controlling does not need to do so.[21] From a traditional controlling perspective, this instrumental view is comprehensible. Yet, this does not meet the aforementioned controller role of being a *change agent*, especially not toward more responsibility.

Remembering the *Corporate Sustainability Barometer*, which claims that controlling is not involved in sustainability topics, the research results of the ICV study show a similar picture with respect to ecology (being one aspect of the triple bottom line). Only 21 corporations out of 295 state that they have a distinct green controlling agenda,[22] which means that the majority does not have a clear-cut picture when it comes to controlling in conjunction with environmental topics. Nevertheless, there is raising awareness of green topics in controlling. The greater part of the respondents sees it as a task for controlling to adapt the existing controlling systems to emerging challenges and admits that the ecological consequences of corporate behavior should be measured and thus be integrated in the steering efforts.[23] Figure 4.2 shows exemplary tasks (and how often they have been mentioned) that the respondents ascribe to an evolving green controlling.

The most important tasks are to be seen in verifying and ensuring the profitability of ecological measures, in monitoring the green target achievement, and in creating transparency for planning and steering through KPIs. The fourth point—actively advising management in terms

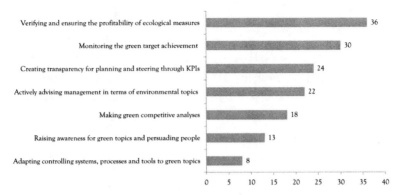

Figure 4.2 Excerpt of green controlling tasks

Source: Reprinted with permission from Internationaler Controller Verein (2011), p. 19.

of environmental topics—reveals that controlling must be a business partner and consultant for environmental matters. The International Controllers Association states that these tasks are not to be seen as new ones. Rather, the existing tasks of controlling must be extended.[24] However, the green controlling movement alone is neglecting the social dimension.

But which existing controlling tasks are suitable and could be extended to sustainability? One possibility is the three steps approach, defined by Günther and Stechemesser, when it comes to green controlling instruments:[25]

- Step 1: Differentiated green controlling (monetary—internal)
- Step 2: Adjusted green controlling (monetary—internal and external)
- Step 3: Extended green controlling (monetary and nonmonetary—internal and external).

In differentiated green controlling (step 1), environmental costs and incomes are shown as separate lines but within the existing accounting realms such as cost centers or cost elements. Günther and Stechemesser ascribe, for instance, activity-based costing, target costing, and life-cycle costing to this step. It is important to note that all aspects are evaluated in monetary terms.[26] Michel points to the recognition of green revenues, which are understood as the percentage of sales achieved with green

Think Outside the Box

Which existing controlling instruments (that you use) could be modified in order to take the triple bottom line into account?

Examples could be target costing, life-cycle costing, cost center accounting, and investment appraisal. What else is coming into your mind?

products. However, what is to be understood as a green product must be defined properly.[27] Adjusted green controlling (step 2) also exclusively considers figures that can be measured on a monetary basis. But in comparison to step 1, also external factors are considered to be important. This step yet again considers life-cycle costing, provided that externalities can be measured monetarily and that they are included into the consideration. Moreover, an abatement costs approach can be mentioned, which quantifies the costs that are needed in order to prevent environmental problems up front.[28] Extended green controlling as the last step includes ecological aspects that cannot be measured financially, for example, the carbon footprint. It tells how many greenhouse gases, reported in so-called CO_2 equivalents, a corporation emits, which is called "organizational carbon footprint,"[29]—or how many CO_2 equivalents are emitted within the life cycle of a product, which is called "product carbon footprint."[30] In the same sense, the water footprint is an instrument of extended green controlling, which measures the amount of water used either by a company in total or within the product life cycle.[31] Consequently, extended green controlling means that controlling is extended from only regarding monetary factors toward the consideration of internal and external monetary and nonmonetary criteria.

Dig Deeper

The nonprofit organization Global Footprint Network informs you about ecological footprints of different types and helps you to get better insights into the footprint discussion:

www.footprintnetwork.org

What cannot be classified concretely into one of the three steps is the evaluation of investments in an integrated—life-cycle thinking—sense. This approach takes economic and ecological factors into account and shows which environmental effects are caused by a decision.[32] Hence, it can be supported by instruments of all three steps. From my viewpoint, evaluating decisions in an integrated way must be part of responsible controlling. Therefore, I return to this topic later.

Sustainability is a complex field with many distinct dimensions. Some experts only focus on the environmental part. In the book *Sustainability Controlling*,[33] it is mostly about energy[34] and topics such as carbon accounting.[35] This indicates a strong focus on environment, even though the title of the book leads to the expectation of a holistic controlling approach in the context of sustainability. Yet, Müller introduces the notion of sociocontrolling and admits that there needs to be a synthesis of all dimensions of sustainability in order to come to sustainability controlling.[36] The following section looks at sociocontrolling or social accounting.

4.2   Sociocontrolling

Within the realm of corporate controlling, sociocontrolling, and consequently adequate instruments, is even less common than green controlling.[37] Strategic controlling instruments may be used for the identification of some social issues, especially by taking into account the relevance of social issues for the stakeholders. With respect to operational controlling, the focus on backward-looking "hard facts"[38] does not give the possibility to cope with changes in a timely manner. In consideration of existing social indicators in controlling, hardly any other criteria than the ones related to employees are referred to. This is not surprising, since gathering internal data about employees seems to be much easier than dealing with stakeholders outside the company, for example.

The topic of sociocontrolling is not new. Ramanathan uses the term corporate social accounting.[39] Remembering that the American management accounting approach is to be understood as being similar to the more European controlling term, I use sociocontrolling and social accounting as synonyms. Social accounting can be defined as "the process of selecting firm-level social performance variables, measures and measurement procedures; systematically developing information useful for evaluating the firm's social performance."[40] Although it is not clearly defined what is to be understood by social performance, Ramanathan mentions two roles of a firm regarding social topics:

- "The delivery of some socially useful goods and services (. . . and)
- The distribution of economic, social or political rewards to social groups from which the firm derives its power."[41]

Think Outside the Box

Have you ever thought about the social performance of your corporation? Which social topics or issues are you addressing? Are you, for example, providing a necessary product to ill people, or are you trying to sell random products?

Especially the first point must not be neglected in the CSR discussion, since delivering socially useful goods and services should actually constitute the corporation's business model. Within contemporary literature, Crane and Matten understand social accounting as a "voluntary process concerned with assessing and communicating organizational activities and impacts on social, ethical, and environmental issues relevant to stakeholders."[42] In my understanding, the environmental part of their definition would rather be a topic of green controlling. Both definitions, Ramanathan's and Crane and Matten's, however, have in common that they do not only regard shareholders, but also the other stakeholders of the corporation. Yet, it is not clear what topics should be regarded: corporations' targets or stakeholders' interests? Moreover, it is to question how social performance as such can be assessed.[43] Nevertheless, it is evident that also in this context, controlling must extend its focus away from being only monetary driven toward the recognition of qualitative information. Having stated that it is not clear what exactly to measure, I now have a look at KPIs in relation to sustainability.

4.3   Key Performance Indicators and Reporting for Sustainability

Earlier, we have learned that, according to an Ernst & Young survey, sustainability reporting is growing but currently not equipped with adequate tools.[44] However, the number of approaches is growing. One of the best-known reporting frameworks, which suggests indicators within the field of sustainability, is issued by the Global Reporting Initiative (GRI). The GRI, a nonprofit, multistakeholder, network-based organization founded in 1997, published its first version of the so-called *Sustainability Reporting Guidelines* in the year 2000.[45] Its latest update—the *G4 Guidelines*—was released in May 2013.[46] The GRI guidelines give directions on how to determine the report content and the report quality. This makes it a very valuable approach for implementers of a sustainability report. Moreover, and for controlling purposes not less relevant, within its standard disclosure, aspects, and indicators with respect to the triple bottom line are suggested, which means within economic, environmental, and social categories. The social part is again subdivided into labor practices and decent work, human rights, society, and product responsibility.[47] Figure 4.3 gives an overview about the topics covered by the *Sustainability Reporting Guidelines*.

Within the three dimensions, one can find the following exemplary indicators.[48]

Regarding the **economic** performance, the direct economic value generated (for example, revenues) and distributed (for example, operating

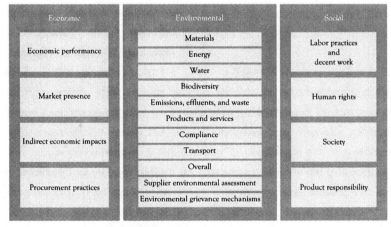

Figure 4.3 Topics covered by GRI guidelines

Source: Reprinted with permission from Global Reporting Initiative, Sustainability Reporting Guidelines—G4—Reporting Principles, and Standard Disclosures, (2013).

costs) are taken into account. In view of the market presence, the proportion of senior management hired from the local community at significant locations of operation is defined as an indicator. With respect to the indirect economic impacts, the development and impact of infrastructure investments and services supported is stated.

In the **environmental** section, indicators are for instance the percentage of materials used that are recycled input materials, the energy consumption within and outside the organization, as well as the percentage and total volume of water recycled and reused.

The **social** part includes type of injury and rates of injury, occupational diseases, lost days and absenteeism, and total number of work-related fatalities, by region and by gender. The percentage and total number of significant investment agreements and contracts that include human rights clauses or that underwent human rights screening and the total number of incidents of discrimination and corrective actions taken.

Dig Deeper

The Global Reporting Initiative provides a good online source with a reasonable overview how a sustainability report should look like and how the reporting process itself should be organized:

g4.globalreporting.org

As can be seen, many of the indicators are of nonmonetary nature. Thus, the GRI framework is an important step toward a comprehensive sustainability understanding—primarily driven by external reporting interests. The *Sustainability Reporting Guidelines* represent a basis for the question which information could be valuable in terms of sustainability. Thurm calls for an approach of implementing only these GRI indicators that are important both internally and externally.[49] GRI G4 names this as materiality. According to the organization, "this new focus on materiality means that sustainability reports will be centered on matters that are really critical in order to achieve the organization's goals and manage its impact on society."[50] For controlling that could mean that the information should not be used if the importance is not given for both views (corporation and stakeholders).[51] Keeping in mind that one should focus on the material aspects, GRI indicators can be a good source for controlling. However, it must be noted that the GRI does not define every indicator in a clear-cut way. Hence, there is latitude regarding the measurement of the data input and therefore comparability is difficult.

Another prevalent concept in the field of sustainability KPIs and reporting is the idea of environmental, social, and governance (ESG) factors. The Society of Investment Professionals in Germany[52] (DVFA), together with the European Federation of Financial Analysts Societies (EFFAS), has developed *Key Performance Indicators for Environmental Social and Governance Issues,* the so-called KPIs for ESG.[53] The two associations define—based on collaboration with different corporations and investors—generally valid factors for all business sectors as well as sector-specific ones.[54] Among others, the following KPIs are seen as crucial: energy efficiency, greenhouse gas emissions in total, staff turnover, litigation risks, and revenues from new products.[55] As can be derived from the KPIs mentioned, such as litigation risks, the KPIs for ESG were especially developed for the purposes of external investors from the capital market.[56] What is said with respect to the GRI indicators is also true for ESG factors: they are externally driven. Whether they meet the requirements for internal controlling is not to be taken for granted in any situation.

The common denominator in both approaches is the circumstance that information from all three dimensions of the triple bottom line is taken into account: economic, environmental, and social aspects. Earlier, we have figured out that the triple bottom line "captures the essence of sustainability by measuring the impact of an organization's activities on the world."[57] Both GRI and ESG demonstrate an effort toward making the triple bottom line transparent. This transparency is important to make the right decision and deduce adequate measures with respect to sustainability.[58] But it is to be noted that reporting is always oriented toward the past and thus is only partly helpful for future decisions. One can claim that it is not sufficient for internal management and controlling to only have the same reporting frequency as external reports,[59] which is normally once per year. Furthermore, only KPIs are helpful for sustainable efforts that are linked to the responsibility of individuals.[60]

Although the International Controllers Association does not cover the full topic of sustainability, it takes into account the measurability of the KPIs in order to make sure that they can serve as a basis for controlling.

Moreover, the association makes a segmentation of its green KPIs by categorizing them into the following classes:[61]

- Input (such as recycling material in relation to total material input)
- Throughput (for example, weight of manufactured products in relation to energy used)
- Output (such as direct and indirect greenhouse gas emissions per product)
- Outcome (for instance, green products sales in relation to total sales).

As can be seen, only relative KPIs are used by the association. This makes sense in order to manage different situations. Yet, relative KPIs do not give a full picture about "an organization's (absolute) activities on the world"[62] and thus cannot exclusively be taken in order to identify whether a corporation really is sustainable. As a reminder: the term sustainable means there are completely no (absolute) negative impacts onto the triple bottom line. Hence, in sustainability management and controlling, you also need to have adequate absolute KPIs in mind.

Although it is difficult to measure CSR, measuring is a crucial tool in order to manage and control it.[63] In controlling, there are normally four criteria for measurement: (1) validity, (2) reliability, (3) objectivity, and (4) efficiency, which should also be valid for sustainability controlling. Validity asks to make sure measuring exactly these factors which are intended to be measured, whereas reliability indicates that one finds the same result if repeating the same measurement. Efficiency must not be ignored: Only if the benefit of measuring something exceeds the costs, controlling should collect this information.[64] Here you could question what exactly is the *benefit*? Profit maximization or being successful in a responsible manner? The third criterion, objectivity, reminds us of the objectivity claimed in decision making.

At this point, we can note, that until so far an ideal method of how controlling can contribute to make a corporation more responsible has not been developed. There are first and valuable efforts with respect to measuring data. However, this is often a very quantitative approach without reflecting the actual way of doing business. The next two sections look at the concept of creating shared value (CSV), which was initially explored by Porter and Kramer.[65] In addition, we examine the notion of corporate social performance[66] in order to clarify whether these concepts can be valuable for responsible controlling.

4.4   Creating Shared Value

Porter and Kramer, inventors of the concept of CSV, understand "shared value (. . . as a principle) which involves creating economic value in a way that *also* creates value for society by addressing its needs and challenges."[67] Hence, businesses can make profits by integrating society's needs in their business processes. Earlier I discussed the business case for CSR, which indicates a similar approach.

The two authors identify three ways of CSV: "by reconceiving products and markets, (by) redefining productivity in the value chain, and (by) building supportive industry clusters at the company's locations."[68] Porter and Kramer show in their paper *The Competitive Advantage of Corporate Philanthropy* that economic and social benefits must not be separated. Instead, they can be combined. Their idea of shared values arises from the realization that "economic and social objectives have long been seen as distinct and often competing. But this is a false dichotomy."[69] Business and society have linkages.

Although that sounds similar to CSR at first glance, Porter and Kramer do not want their concept to be understood as CSR, but as "a new way to achieve economic success."[70] They argue that CSV "is not on the margin of what companies do but at the center."[71] If once again we recall the description of what is to be understood by CSR that argumentation is surprising. Earlier I have concluded that CSR is related to the integration of responsibility into the business operations and its core strategy. Even though Porter's and Kramer's concept is very helpful when it comes to bringing societal aspects into the companies' boardrooms, I will not fully follow this approach. I already see CSR as being at the center of what companies should do and therefore we follow the CSR and corporate sustainability approach.

From a uniquely and exclusively economic perspective, CSV may make sense. After all, value in an economic sense can be created by taking societal factors into account, that is, by creating value for the society.[72] A similar concept is Prahalad's model of the bottom of the pyramid. According to him, the "bottom of the pyramid" markets represent the four to five billion poor people who are mostly neglected by the multinational firms.[73] If companies care about their needs, they could also improve their financial bottom line and also from my standpoint that cannot be seen as reprehensible. Companies must focus on the interrelations between themselves and society and business decisions must be valuable for both of them. A social understanding must, hence, be integrated into the corporation's strategy.[74] From a CSV perspective, companies must only concentrate on the social issues that also create shared value for themselves, that is, focusing on the issues that are to be seen as business opportunities and hence as an investment into the long-term viability of the corporation.[75] CSV "is not philanthropy but self-interested behavior to create economic value by creating societal value."[76] That is to be seen as an egoist instrumental ethics approach, which means that only those issues are addressed with which a company can make profits. However, we must recognize that it is a realistic approach with respect to a corporation's own resources. Instead of losing sight due to an overwhelming range of issues, Porter and Kramer's approach stresses to focus on the topics that the company can address best to serve society's needs.[77] If that circumstance would be based on an ethical basis, it could be a valuable thought of steering a company toward more responsibility and thus help to establish responsible controlling. Even the two authors realize that the "purpose of the corporation must be redefined as creating shared value, not just profit per se."[78] Yet, it is hardly to be perceived as something else than an instrumental understanding since they additionally see CSV as "integral to profit maximization."[79] Hence, their arguments are contradictory to some extent. Within the framework of this book, the unmodified concept of CSV is perceived as being too instrumental. Yet, the link to controlling comes into play, when Porter and Kramer realize that "concrete and tailored metrics"[80] are necessary for CSVs.

4.5   Corporate Social Performance

Another term in the realm of sustainability and corporate behavior is that of corporate social performance (CSP). In conjunction with this term,

Carroll is to be mentioned again. Earlier we have seen how he defines social responsibility: as encompassing "the economic, legal, ethical, and discretionary expectations that society has of organizations at a given point of time."[81] Moreover, we have experienced that CSR is to be seen in relation to the *social issues* involved. For Carroll, social responsibilities and social issues are two dimensions of corporate social performance. In his paper *A Three-Dimensional Conceptual Model of Corporate Performance*, he adds a third dimension: "social responsiveness,"[82] which is to be understood as the "(managerial) response to social responsibility and social issues."[83] Carroll describes four possibilities of social responsiveness that can be understood as a continuum: (1) reaction, (2) defense, (3) accommodation, and (4) proaction.[84] The first dimension—reaction—means that a company only reacts to social pressure, while the fourth one—proaction—indicates that it is dealing proactively with the responsibilities, if appropriate at best, before the issue arises. Putting social responsibility, social issues, and social responsiveness together, Carroll develops a three-dimensional conceptual model of corporate performance. For him, "social performance requires that (1) a firm's social responsibility be assessed, (2) the social issues it must address be identified, and (3) a response philosophy be chosen."[85]

Carroll is not the only one using the term of corporate social performance. Several papers have been published regarding the link of CSP and a company's financial success. Nevertheless, empirical evidence cannot be found that a good social performance positively influences corporate financial performance in any case.[86] Raghubir, Roberts, Lemon, and Winer formulate it as follows:[87]

> After 36 years, 167 studies, and 16 reviews of the relationship between CSR and financial performance, the answer to the debate about whether CSR is profitable is unambiguously clear: "It depends."

One of the problems is to be seen in the fact that CSP is hard to measure, since CSP consists of several dimensions.[88] Also, Carroll points to the fact that he discusses a conceptual framework. He does not give clear-cut instructions on how to measure CSP.[89] Hence, we can note that also the concept of CSP is a valuable concept for us and you may want to dig a little deeper. However, it cannot just be taken without alteration in order to establish responsible controlling.

4.6   Some Points to Remember

- Controlling must extend its mostly financial focus onto ecological and social factors. In that sense, it is important to integrate social and environmental topics into the existing controlling functions and systems instead of creating a separated sustainability controlling view.
- Currently, green controlling as well as sociocontrolling approaches are being developed.
- The GRI offers the best-known methodology when it comes to sustainability reporting and to finding material KPIs.
- When talking about CSV we remember that it is important that a corporation focuses on the issues it can address best to serve society's needs.
- CSP is hard to measure and there is still no profound evidence that behaving responsibly pays off in monetary terms.

CHAPTER 5

Responsible Controlling: Synthesizing Controlling and Responsible Management

"Management, like the combustion engine, is a mature technology that must now be reinvented for a new age."[1]

—Gary Hamel

Ethical Issues Are Not That Far

Remember the ResCoCo example which must improve its bottom line? How have you decided? Have you suggested to lay off your friend who has a family with kids? Or have you proposed to change the supplier and thus accepted possible human rights infringements? For all these ethical questions there is clearly no right or wrong. However, there may be better or worse decisions. You could, for example, think about implementing an up-to-date product range within the existing business unit and thus make the unit profitable again, preferably with ecologically friendly and socially desirable products.

Our vision is responsible controlling, which is aware of these dilemmas. The assumption of responsibility is deeply rooted in every controlling function. Controlling is a driver toward corporate responsibility and focuses on positively influencing the triple bottom line. Ethics as a reflection effort is the basis for every action. Morality, legitimacy, and justice are regular approaches in daily controlling behavior. The following tools and steps shall help you with that.

5.1   Is It Necessary to Call for Responsible Controlling?—A Critical Reflection of the Status Quo

So far, we have evaluated what is to be understood by *controlling*, how does controlling look like in concrete terms, and what are the current trends in controlling with respect to sustainability and responsibility. Even though some good approaches have been shown that attempt to interlink controlling and distinct realms of corporate social responsibility (CSR), the question is whether the prevalent controlling trends are sufficient when it comes to responsibility. It is to ask whether the controlling trends elaborated earlier are appropriate to make controlling a driver toward a more responsible company. We need to be skeptical about the holism of the approaches and about the degree of implementation within existing controlling departments. Therefore, Table 5.1 gives a first overview about the sufficiency of the discussed approaches with respect to several attributes that are perceived as being important for a responsible company.

The attributes have been derived from the discussion about responsibility earlier within this book. I deliberately refrain from using a classical scoring model that attaches weights to the different attributes with the aim of bringing them in an order. As we have seen, the field of CSR is very complex and thus it cannot easily be determined which attributes are the most important ones. However, I draw attention to the fact that responsible controlling should take ethical aspects as a basis. Moreover, it is relevant if the approach helps to steer a corporation, whether it is integrated in existing systems and into core processes and if the actual behavior is critically reflected in a way that controlling plays a role of a change maker.

As can be seen, none of the discussed approaches meets all of the outlined requirements that I derive from the elaborations within the past chapters. The concept that integrates all of the prerequisites will be called **responsible controlling**.

The rightmost column illustrates how I picture the prototype of responsible controlling.

As a consequence of the unmet characteristics, I can state that the status quo of controlling and reporting approaches is not comprehensively sufficient when it comes to CSR. However, I want to strongly

Table 5.1 Analysis: sufficiency to make an organization more responsible

Criteria		Traditional controlling	Green controlling	Sociocontrolling	KPIs and reporting	Creating shared value	Corporate social performance	Responsible controlling
Ethical approach	Consequentialist	x	x	x	x	x	x	x
	Nonconsequentialist							x
Target	Profit maximization	x	x			x		
	Based on morality			(x)	(x)		x	x
Stakeholder approach	Based on acceptance	x	x	(x)	x	x		
	Based on legitimacy				(x)		(x)	x
Justice	Intergenerational		(x)	(x)	(x)		(x)	x
	Intragenerational		(x)	(x)	(x)		(x)	x
Holistic approach	Internal	x	x	x	x	x	x	x
	External (including supply chain)			x	x	x	x	x
Focus and transparency on triple bottom line	Ecology			x		x	(x)	x
	Economy	x			x	x		x
	Society			x	x	(x)	x	x
Relevance for steering a corporation	KPIs and KPI system	x	x	x	x			x
	Support for decision making	x	x	x	(x)			x
	Derivation of measures	x	(x)	(x)	(x)	(x)		x
Integration	... in existing systems	x	x	x	(x)			x
	... in core business processes and strategy	x	x	x	(x)	x		x
Controlling as change maker	Critical reflection of actual economic situation?					(x)	x	x
Sufficiency to make an organization more responsible								x

Note: How to read this table?
  x = the respective approach is perceived as being supportive for responsible controlling.
Blank = no positive contribution is perceived.
  (x) = requirements are only partly met.

state that the existing approaches are providing an excellent basis on which to rely on. Therefore, it should definitely be recommended to use the existing approaches and adapt and merge them when it comes to making controlling responsible. It would be nonsense not making use of established, well-known approaches with which the controlling and accounting community is familiar.

Dig Deeper

If you are a student in a business school this may be an interesting research topic. Table 5.1 shows what I perceive as being relevant within the business world. However, further research about which approach brings what contribution would be of high interest.

Earlier we have seen that sustainability is concerned with balancing economic, ecological, and social aspects. Moreover, we have understood that the different controlling approaches cover all aspects to some extent—finance being the prevalent one. A comprehensive, balanced controlling framework that comprises all views at the same time is missing, as shown in Table 5.1. Furthermore, in order to establish controlling as a driver toward responsibility, *not only sustainability metrics should be controlled, but controlling itself should take responsibility, sustainability, and ethics into account* when defining targets, identifying stakeholders, and helping to make decisions. If that were given, controlling itself would be sustainable or better: *responsible*.

At this point, I want to recall my assertion:

Responsible controlling is indispensable to make an organization more responsible.

Before going ahead with defending this claim, I summarize the findings by answering several questions:

- **Why is controlling important at all?**
  Because it helps to make decisions on a (instrumentally) rational basis by bringing transparency into the decision making process in order to avoid managers' subjectivity.
- **Why should controlling play an important role in efforts to make an organization more responsible and thus be indispensable?**
  Because controlling has a cross-departmental function, it is at a key position to establish responsible thinking throughout the organization—from purchasing departments to sales functions. If controlling does not change the understanding of its own role (from only being monetary driven toward a

holistic thinking) it is hard to establish responsibility within a company. Responsibility would always be questioned from a profit-*maximization* viewpoint and be seen as a threat to efficiency.

- **Is the status quo of controlling approaches sufficient to establish responsibility?**

  No, it is not as shown in Table 5.1. Therefore, I strongly call for a responsible controlling approach. However, the different existing approaches are a very valuable basis on which the transformation toward more responsibility should be based.

- **Does controlling still have a right to exist when it comes to responsibility?**

  Yes, if controlling is understood in a broader sense. The triple bottom line implies a financial view. Furthermore, it is necessary that controlling—understood as management support toward good performance—is also performed in the social and ecological dimension. Controlling needs to make sure that economic, ecological, and social targets are reached.

5.2   A Framework and a Roadmap toward Responsible Controlling

Hamel claims that "management, like the combustion engine, is a mature technology that must now be reinvented for a new age."[2] Remembering the interconnection between managers and controllers, we realize that what Hamel asserts with respect to management is also true for controlling. At the beginning of this book, I have revealed the issue that controlling departments are hardly involved in sustainability and that they do not contribute to corporate responsibility. Based on that, within the framework of this book, it is my aim to reinvent controlling in such a way that it can become a driver toward sustainability. When the question is raised on how responsible controlling can be implemented, we must realize that there are already several attempts toward making controlling involved in sustainable thinking. The different concepts have been delineated earlier. With respect to the target of this book, I synthesize the notions of controlling and responsibility. Hence, I take the prevalent concepts and merge them to a holistic controlling framework. At this point, *ethics* is coming into play again—by establishing a *reflection* process.

I present a responsible controlling framework, which takes into account all three dimensions of sustainability, but which has a clear fundament: an ethical understanding. The necessary tools, particularly with respect to KPIs, are currently being developed by different institutions and authors. Think, for example, about the Global Reporting Initiative or the Green Controlling movement. Subsequently, we, first of all, take into consideration the "**how**": how to implement a controlling function and a controlling understanding in order to perform its (extended) tasks on a responsible fundament and thus make your company more responsible? How to synthesize controlling and responsible management?

In short, I illustrate a roadmap and outline a recommended course of action on how to realize responsible controlling. The focus of this endeavor is put on the operational benefit for your organization.

Different approaches of a synthesized understanding of responsibility and controlling could be envisaged. For example, the following:

a. Implementation of a new controlling function called **responsibility controlling**, which exclusively deals with the topics of sustainability and responsibility, that is, taking especially the ecological and social part of the triple bottom line into account by implementing new controlling instruments in order to extend the actual (monetary) observation toward a holistic view.

b. Putting responsibility into every action of controlling. That means not installing merely responsibility controlling as a function, but also integrating responsible thinking into controlling in general. That would be **responsible controlling**.

Earlier we have seen the controlling cycle and the controlling process model (Section 3.2). We figured out that both of them will help us to conceptualize a roadmap toward responsible controlling. The subsequently discussed topics of the roadmap from step 3—Analysis of the status quo (Section 6.3) until step 9—consideration of stakeholders (Section 7.2) can be classified into the controlling process of *strategic planning*. This part deals with examining vision, mission, values, and the underlying business model, as well as with including stakeholders into the strategy development. The processes of *cost accounting* and *management reporting* comprise the data platform (Section 7.4) and the process of *project controlling* implies decision making (Section 7.6). As outlined earlier, we now realize that the controlling processes are not mutually exclusive. Hence, I can state the following: for the responsible controlling framework, it is important that we have understood the link to the well-known controlling process model. That makes it easier for controllers to understand the responsible controlling effort. In the following, I outline a roadmap with different consecutive steps toward responsibility that cross through several controlling processes. The attempt of establishing responsible controlling can best be classified into the process of *enhancement of organisation, processes, instruments and systems*, which in turn influences all other processes.

Eschenbach and Siller use the barely known expression of normative controlling as an addition to strategic and operative controlling.[3] As we see now, this type of controlling indicates the direction of this book. Stra-

Normative Controlling

- raises the question if your and your company's behavior is ethically correct;
- focuses heavily on reflection.

tegic controlling asks about *doing the right things* and operational controlling about *doing the things right*. Normative controlling raises the question whether the corporate behavior is ethically correct[4] and thus introduces a completely new type of question into controlling thinking. While I described the tools of strategic and operative controlling symbolically as telescope and microscope, respectively, the tool of normative controlling is to be seen in reflection.[5] You may now realize why you have found some reflection boxes (*think outside the box*) in the course of this book: in order to make you familiar with the main aspect of normative controlling.

What is not clearly outlined in most normative controlling approaches is the interconnection of the three types of controlling. However, you have figured out earlier that in practice there is no clear-cut distinction between strategic and operational controlling. Hence, I do not consider it as sufficient to simply put a normative controlling alongside them.

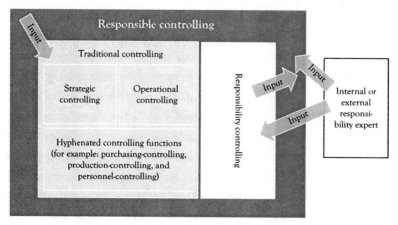

Figure 5.1 Conceptual framework of a responsible controlling

Therefore, in my understanding, responsible controlling should be constructed as shown in Figure 5.1. From the conceivable approaches of

a. implementation of a new controlling function (**responsibility controlling**), which exclusively deals with the topics of responsibility; and

b. putting responsibility into every action of controlling, which means installing **responsible controlling**, I take both into account.

Responsible controlling is the desired condition, the end state of an ethically, sustainably, and responsibly behaving controlling. In other words, it is a synthesis of responsible management and controlling. The responsibility controlling function, on the other hand, helps to establish responsibility at all. In the following, I build up this framework step by step and, thus, I recommend a course of action on how practitioners could set up responsible controlling, based on the thoroughly examined background.

Figure 5.2 gives you an overview of the responsible controlling roadmap.

In Chapters 6 and 7, I show you in detail how you could set up responsible controlling. For this, I use two stages:

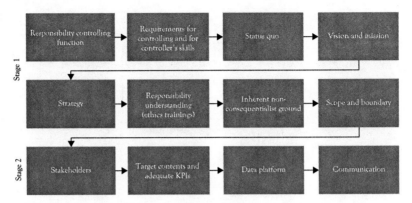

Figure 5.2 Responsible controlling roadmap

- Stage 1: Soft factors and people (from *Responsibility controlling function* until *Inherent nonconsequentialist ground*)
- Stage 2: Hard factors and structures (from *Scope and boundary* until *Communication*).

If your focus lies on soft factors and people, read Chapter 6 closely. If you are mainly interested in hard factors and structure, it is recommended to pay attention to Chapter 7. However, I urge reading both stages to get a holistic understanding of responsible controlling.

CHAPTER 6

Stage 1: Soft Factors and People

"Action comes, not from thought, but from a readiness for responsibility."[1]

—Dietrich Bonhoeffer

6.1 Step 1: Acknowledgment to the Installation of a Responsibility Controlling Function

The first step within the effort of establishing controlling as a driver toward responsibility is the installation of a person or a controlling subdivision that is in charge of dealing with this topic. This is a very important action. With this decision, the head of controlling or the management board shows a first commitment toward sustainability. The Ernst & Young survey shown earlier stated that the chief financial officer (CFO) is gaining an important role in sustainability topics.[2] To ensure that she or he has the right knowledge and that she or he can make well-informed decisions, it is essential for her or him to have a controller or a controlling team who supports her or him in terms of responsibility and sustainability. Furthermore, we have learned that it is important to have the necessary "execution capabilities"[3] to become a pioneer within the megatrend of sustainability. From that we can derive the following questions:

- Does your organization give sufficient time for responsibility thinking to the person(s) in charge, aiming at not overstraining the person(s) by seeing sustainability only as an additional topic, done in addition to "normal" business?

- Do you choose or have you chosen someone who either possesses the necessary skills of controlling and responsibility or someone who is willing to acquire the missing skills within a short period of time?

As Bonhoeffer says "action comes, not from thought, but from a readiness for responsibility."[4] So it is up to you as a controller to develop responsible thinking within your organization. Also if you are a manager it is up to you: Do you transform your readiness for responsibility into an action by installing a responsibility controller? The question for you may be whether it is more reasonable to pick an internal employee or one coming from outside the company, or even a consultant. This issue may not be answered in an unambiguous way. Yet, we have figured out that controlling is highly dependent on interrelations between employees of several corporate functions and that coordination is a main task of controlling. From this viewpoint, the new responsibility tasks can probably be performed more appropriately by a person who already has an existing network within the organization. This network is helpful in establishing that person as a role model toward responsibility. I therefore argue for the following approach.

Installing an *internal person as a responsibility controller*. But since this person—most likely a controller who has an educational background in management—may not be completely proficient in the topic of responsibility, he or she should be trained by an (external) responsibility expert, if applicable. Eschenbach and Siller stress that controllers will not be experts in ethics, but that they are moderators and help to solve conflicts in contemporary controller's practice.[5] The (internal or external) responsibility expert, however, does not have the network inside the company. Instead, he or she brings the missing knowledge and coaches your internal controller on a regular basis. Owing to that constellation, I ensure that the input into the responsible controlling framework is coming from both the (internal) controlling side and an ethical perspective.

The responsibility controller (and his or her responsibility counterpart, if necessary) is in charge of developing the responsible controlling framework, which, after its completion, permeates every controlling function, no matter if divided in operational, strategic, or in distinct hyphenated controlling areas. He or she has to coordinate the implementation of responsibility into the (controlling) processes, to develop adequate tools based on his or her methodological competences, and to offer training to his or her controlling coworkers, to managers, and to every other person who is involved in decision making. And what is the aim? If upon completion of the responsible controlling framework, responsible thinking is entirely realized throughout your organization, the responsibility controlling function would make itself redundant. That would be the perfect state. So what does that mean for ResCoCo? Assuming that ResCoCo's management board is interested in transforming its business into a responsible one, above all, it is necessary that they are willing to install a person who is in charge of integrating responsibility, sustainability, and ethics into controlling and from there on into the whole organization. Some simple questions may help (please have a look at the following box).

Think Outside the Box

- Is there a top management commitment toward sustainability within your organization?
- Has your organization realized the necessity to appoint someone who is in charge of implementing responsibility thinking into controlling?
- Is your organization willing to give enough time to this person in order to perform his or her task well?
- Have you made sure that the appointed person is both interested and has the necessary skills regarding responsibility, sustainability, and ethics? If not, have you chosen a counterpart from the responsibility, sustainability, and ethics side who supports the responsibility controller?
- And last but not least, does this person have adequate access and connections to the management board?

6.2   Step 2: Requirements for Controlling and for Controllers' Skills

After having acknowledged the importance of appointing a person in charge and after having defined on a general level what this person needs to do, the next step—before really installing someone to this position—is to define the requirements regarding responsibility controlling as a function and regarding the skills of the controller in charge.

6.2.1   General Requirements of a Responsible Controlling Function

With respect to controlling as a function, the general requirements—deduced from the elaborations herein—are to be seen as the following:

- Both a nonconsequentialist and a consequentialist ethics approach should be taken into consideration when executing controlling tasks.
- Profit maximization must not be seen as an end in itself; instead, corporate targets (in whose agreement controlling is permanently involved) must be based on morality.
- Stakeholder identification needs to take into account the legitimacy of the claims.
- There are two dimensions of justice that need to be considered: intergenerational and intragenerational justice.
- The responsible controlling framework must be holistic, both in terms of taking internal and external factors into account and in terms of bringing transparency into the organization's triple bottom line.
- The approach must help management to steer the company by using KPIs in order to make decisions and derive measures.
- Integration into existing systems is to be aspired.
- Controlling should critically reflect the actual way of doing its business.

6.2.2   Controller's Skills With Respect to Responsibility

Eschenbach and Siller mention skills for controllers that match with my controlling approach. According to them, controllers should have a *"personal imagination of ethics."*[6] Not exactly outlining what *personal* means, they add, that a controller should be a role model in terms of *being objective* and in terms of *being aware of the consequences* of his or her acting. This also includes assuming responsibility. Moreover, they ascribe the attributes of *critically and neutrally reflecting the status quo* and *initiating reasonable change* to controllers. What is also important is *self-criticism.* A controller must as well be *open-minded* toward learning something new and must be proactive. The just-mentioned points belong to personal attributes. With respect to social competences, they mention the necessity to be a *team player* and to *openly communicate*, as well as to realize that *trust,* which needs to be gained again and again, is very important when it comes to controlling.[7] Remembering that Suchanek sees the retention of trustworthiness as the actual corner stone of a corporation's *responsibility,*[8] we realize another link of controlling and corporate social responsibility (CSR). Related to sustainability controlling, Müller mentions that it is a change process, for which it is indispensable for controllers to be a trustworthy role model and a change agent.[9] Moreover, he states that controlling must be aware of the fact that it is **easier to change methods than people's behavior.**[10] This is important for you to realize. On your way toward responsible controlling, it is not only the tools and methods that count. Rather, **it is the people and personalities with their different mindsets that are crucial for the success or failure of making your organization more responsible**.

Derived from the results obtained earlier, I add the following skills needed in order to be a responsible controller. Having an *understanding of ethics*, which means not making its own ethics, is one of the most crucial points. That is one reason why we had a thorough look at ethics within the responsibility chapter. Only with the knowledge about the pluralism of ethics approaches, a controller will be able to regard his or her action from different perspectives—taking morality, legitimacy of stakeholder claims, and the dimensions of justice into consideration. Furthermore, a responsible controller should *be aware of the triple bottom line approach* and realize that decisions most likely affect every dimension, not only the economic one. Hence, what is very important is a *joined-up thinking* in order to integrate responsible topics into the current controlling processes.

With respect to the responsible controlling framework, it is the target that each and every controller is a responsible controller and thus he or she should have these characteristics and skills. However, at the beginning, it is essential that at least the responsibility controller, who introduces the topic, is equipped with them. ResCoCo, our exemplary company, wants to install a sustainability controller. Now it is up to the board and most likely to the head of controlling and to the human resources department to figure out if somebody within the company has the aforementioned skills or if somebody is interested in doing the job and developing the skills.

Think Outside the Box

- Does your organization have a controller with the mentioned skills?
- Are you willing to develop these skills or are you willing to have somebody develop these skills?
- Is your organization ready to realize that tools are important, but that responsible controlling first and foremost means to change mindsets and behaviors?

6.3   Step 3: Analysis of the Status Quo

Once the responsibility controller is appointed and it is clarified whether an external expert is needed, an analysis of the current corporate controlling behavior needs to be carried out with respect to responsibility. In other words, a critical reflection of the actual way of executing controlling is to be made, extended by general responsibility questions. To do so, I suggest a questionnaire (shown in Table 6.1) that is based on the sufficiency analysis, but which focuses on practical issues instead of theoretical aspects.

With the intention of both reflecting upon controllers' self-perception and of getting to know their image within the organization, the questionnaire should be filled in by controllers and by the stakeholders. However, now we realize an alleged inconsistency within the roadmap. Earlier, I had mentioned that the legitimacy of the claims is the decisive factor when it comes to the identification of stakeholders. Not neglecting this

Table 6.1 Questionnaire of current controlling approach

	Criterion	Exemplary answers
Corporate questions	Is CSR a topic at all within the organization?	Yes/no
	Is there a top management commitment toward CSR?	Yes/no
	If yes, is the awareness broken down into the organization?	Yes/no
Controlling questions	Is there an internal controller vision and mission statement?	Yes/no
	What are the underlying responsibilities of controlling?	Profit maximization versus morality
	Is decision making driven by targets or by good intentions?	Monetary targets/reasonable arguments
	What are the most important KPIs? Are they only of monetary nature?	Profit/sales/efficiency/number of accidents/CO_2 emissions
	Are IT systems used for supporting management?	Yes/no
	What is controlling's reputation within the organization?	Number cruncher/narrow-minded change agent/open-minded
	Are controllers trusted by managers and employees?	Yes/no
	What is the scope of controlling tasks?	Internal/external; triple bottom line aspects
	Which stakeholders are taken into consideration?	Managers/employees/suppliers
	Is there installed a green controlling or socio-controlling or are GRI or ESG factors used?	Yes/no
	Have there been moral dilemmas that were recognized in the past?	Yes/no
	If yes, which ones?	Child labor vs. profit maximization
	If no, is the awareness for dilemmas missing?	Yes/no
	Have controllers been trained in ethical aspects?	Yes/no
	What is controllers' educational background?	Study in finance/engineering/sociology

fact, for the purpose of getting a first overview of the current controlling approach, I propose taking the management as stakeholders into consideration. The reason is to be seen in the fact that the survey does not deal primarily with claims and does not imply decision making, but attempts to screen the status quo. Managers, as the counterpart of controllers in executing *controlling*, are most likely the ones who have most insights into controlling besides the controllers themselves.

Doubtless, the raised questions represent a proposal. In our context, I derived it from the elaborations herein. They could be altered in your day-to-day practice to better match the situation of the respective organization. Moreover, I deliberately refrain from judging about *good* or *bad* answers. The questionnaire intends to get a first impression of controlling within your organization. If, for example, ResCoCo's managers state that they do not trust the controllers, it is an indicator that there are some personal and organizational issues that probably need to be clarified before installing sustainability KPIs. In case there is an answer that moral dilemmas have not been recognized in the past, the controller in charge may raise the question, why not? Have there really been no dilemmas (we will have a look at dilemmas later) or have they not been noticed? Remember the predicament at ResCoCo: either dismissing people or accepting to be complicit in human rights abuses. Obviously, there have been moral dilemmas in the past. But probably these dilemmas have not been realized since there was no awareness of the nonfinancial parts of the triple bottom line.

However, what is more important than the single questions and answers themselves is the circumstance that making this analysis brings a (first) awareness of the link between controlling and responsibility into the respondents' mindset.

Think Outside the Box

- Have you already asked questions like you find in Table 6.1?
- If not, reflect your own controlling by bringing the questionnaire or parts of it into use within your organization!
- Which conclusions can you draw from the answers?

6.4 Step 4: Definition of a Vision and Creation of a Controlling Mission Statement

A "clear vision"[11] is crucial in order to be a pioneer within the sustainability megatrend. Consequently, once the status quo is analyzed, it is helpful to define a responsible controlling vision and to create a mission statement for a responsible controlling. A vision defines "what or where the organization wants to be."[12] It represents "an image . . . in the future that motivates employees to focus their actions toward a common point."[13] Since this book should support you no matter in which kind of organization you are active, I do not take a specific corporate vision into consideration—what might be very helpful in your corporate practice—but define an own responsible controlling vision:

Responsible Controlling Vision

My vision for responsible controlling is that responsibility is deeply rooted in every controlling function. Controlling is a driver toward responsibility and focuses on positively influencing the triple bottom line. Ethics as a reflection effort is the basis for every action. Morality, legitimacy, and justice are regular approaches in daily controlling behavior.

According to Gill, an "organization's mission defines why the organization exists and what it does. . . . A mission is a practical way of putting a vision into action."[14] Following that, a *controlling* mission statement must therefore define what controlling is doing and what is the reason for its existence, showing "what are the values, beliefs and guiding principles."[15] The following sections show you a responsible controlling value and mission statement referring to the one from the International Group of Controlling but basing it on an ethical fundament, including the aforementioned requirements. The value statement underlines what values are necessary to contribute to the responsible controlling vision. The mission statement shows the practical right for the existence of responsible controlling and explains why responsible controlling is needed and is even needed in case that ethical thinking is not yet prevalent in your organization so far—or like in the ResCoCo example.

Responsible Controlling Value and Mission Statement

Value Statement

Responsible controllers

- are aware of ethical approaches and recognize ethical dilemmas;
- are accustomed to both principle-based reasoning and the consideration of consequences;
- acknowledge the unimpeachable human dignity and realize that legitimacy has priority over profit maximization;
- are conscious of the triple bottom line and thus are committed to society as a whole.

Mission Statement

Responsible controllers

- ensure transparency within the organization's triple bottom line and provide managers with all relevant controlling information;
- support managers toward ethical decision taking together with the stakeholders affected;
- contribute to a holistic understanding and to the integration of responsibility into the business operations and its core strategy;
- are devoted to the future and therefore reveal opportunities and risks for both the organization and the stakeholders;
- design and moderate the controlling process of defining goals, planning, and management control;
- organize an integrated sustainability reporting system that is future-oriented and covers the enterprise and its stakeholders as a whole.

Think Outside the Box

- Has your organization already established a controlling vision and mission and does it comprise ethical thinking?
- What is the image of your controlling you picture in the future?
- What is the reason of the existence of your controlling department?

6.5   Step 5: Definition of a Strategy

Earlier, we have seen that the characteristics of green controlling, as understood by the International Controllers Association, range from a holistic green strategy to green compliance.[16] I have declared the ICV understanding as an instrumental one, since it acknowledges that the green controlling approach has to fit the strategic importance of environmental factors for the organization. If there is no such importance, green controlling, according to this understanding, would not be required at all. The responsible controlling approach, alternatively, rests on a different ground. It is not only about supporting management in order to achieve business purposes. Instead, responsible controlling means that controlling is a critical change agent to make a company more sustainable. This does not mean that monetary profitability is not an aim, besides others. With respect to controlling's strategy, I therefore argue for the following: if controlling itself should be responsible, it must set up a strategy on how to integrate responsibility throughout the controlling realm and throughout the organization. In case responsibility is not yet a primary component of the corporate strategy, controlling needs to make sure that the responsibility vision is becoming an integrated part of the overall corporate strategy.

A strategy "determines how the organization is going to undertake its mission."[17] In our case, it asks how the responsible controlling vision and mission can be turned into practice. Since we have already realized that responsibility has to do with mindsets and controlling has mainly to do with figures, I picture the strategy as shown in Figure 6.1.

This strategy, hence, needs to represent a healthy mix of mindsets and figures. Within the next steps of the roadmap, I depict more precisely how a responsible controlling strategy looks like. It is shown in detail, how I

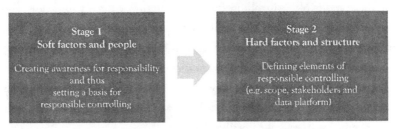

Figure 6.1 Overview of the responsible controlling strategy

envisage turning the vision and mission into reality. As you may have realized, in the process of this book, we are already in the middle of stage 1.

For your day-to-day work as a business practitioner you might want to define your strategy more precisely. I would highly appreciate it if you want to share it with me. Regarding ResCoCo's responsible controlling efforts, it is to assume that they are on a good way. At this point they have already dealt with soft factors like the needed skills and the vision and we assume that they have also undertaken a status quo analysis

Think Outside the Box

- How do you think your responsible controlling vision can best be integrated into your organizational practice?
- Do you have the power and courage to talk about responsibility, sustainability, and ethics—although it is not an order from the management board?

6.6   Step 6: Development of a Responsibility Understanding Through Training

I demand an awareness of ethical approaches and the recognition of ethical dilemmas within controlling functions. Hence, we must provide the opportunity to controllers to acquire knowledge in terms of ethics. It is to say that—after now having developed a vision and mission statement and drafted a brief strategy—it is important to establish responsibility training for controllers. Most likely in order to do so, an internal or external responsibility expert is needed. After completion of installing the responsible controlling framework within your organization, the responsibility controller, him or herself, may conduct the training. This chapter argues for three aspects of responsibility training: (1) establishing a common knowledge base about sustainability, ethics, and responsibility, (2) getting accustomed to the thought of ethics in decision making (the decision making tool itself will be developed later; see Section 7.6), and (3) creating awareness for possible dilemmas.

6.6.1   Establishment of a Basic Responsibility Understanding

The following aspects should be covered in the training:

- Responsibility and sustainability in an organizational context
- Why should an organization assume responsibility—profit or morality?
- What responsibilities does an organization have?

Recalling Chapter 2, *Responsibility, Sustainability, and Ethics,* the aforementioned topics have been thoroughly elaborated in this book. In case you have skipped these points earlier, you may now go back and dig a little deeper. At this point, I will just sum up the basic content. *Responsibility and sustainability in an organizational context* makes the controller aware of the terms of corporate (social)

Think Outside the Box

- Challenge yourself: what do you still remember from our discussions about responsibility?
- Have you already asked and answered some of the questions you have found in the boxes in order to get a better understanding of the (ir-) responsible behavior of your organization? What have been the outcomes?

responsibility, sustainability, and the triple bottom line. Moreover, Barbier's Venn diagram is introduced, which will be relevant to us later on. The question of *why a company should assume responsibility—profit or morality*—deals with the overall topic of ethics. The controller will get to know different consequentialist and nonconsequentialist ethics approaches. He or she will learn about morality, justice, and legitimacy. When dealing with the question *what responsibilities does a company have*, responsibilities that are based on legitimate claims throughout the triple bottom line of the organization are discussed. Within the training sessions, no clear-cut way on how to behave will be discussed. Rather, it is the goal to make the controller aware of ethics and of the prism of the different ethics approaches that will help him or her to regard decisions from distinct perspectives. With this, he or she becomes accustomed to take into account nonprofit-maximizing aspects.

6.6.2   Introduction of Ethics Into Decision Making

In the previous step of training I have introduced the basics of responsibility. Now, with respect to decision making, a first understanding of the link between ordinary controlling thinking and ethics should be created within the training. Carroll alleges that "moral issues in management are not isolated and distinct from traditional business decision making but right smack in the middle of it. . . . Therefore, *moral* competence is an integral part of *managerial* competence."[18] He argues for an integration of "managerial and moral competence."[19] In his paper *In Search of the Moral Manager*, Carroll claims that "a sense of moral obligation (is the) foundation for all (managerial) capacities."[20] While he is talking about *managers*, I transfer his statement to controllers, too.

Moral obligation reminds us of deontological ethics (you may want to have a look again into Section 2.2). Yet, decision making toward target achievement—as normally done in business—is rather to be classified as teleological ethics. Further on in this chapter, I use the ethics approaches discussed earlier in order to create a proposal for ethical decision making specifically for controlling. But, first, an ethical decision making model should be considered while training for the sake of creating awareness and understanding among controllers regarding the meaning of ethical decision making:[21]

1. Recognizing moral issue
2. Making moral judgment
3. Establishing moral intent
4. Engaging in moral behavior.

Jones sees four steps in ethical decision making. After the possible *moral issue* (1) is recognized, a *moral judgment* (2) has to be made. Then, the *moral intent* (3) is established, before the actual *moral behavior* (4) is implemented.[22] All steps are dependent on the moral intensity and partly on organizational factors, such as authority issues. Moral intensity in Jones' understanding contains, for example, the magnitude of consequences, the probability of the effect, and temporal immediacy.[23] Paying attention to consequences points out that the decision making model is to a certain extent related to consequentialist ethics.

I agree with Jones' model and think it is valuable to discuss it with controllers in order to bring a different perspective into a controller's mind. Nevertheless, I aim at introducing a model that is more tangible for a controller's practice (my own more detailed elaboration will be synthesized in Section 7.6). Within the training, six steps of the Ethics Resource Center regarding general decision making should be introduced next:[24]

1. Definition of the problem, what includes the identification of the desired condition (the target), and the realization of gaps between the actual and the desired state.
2. Identification of (more than two) alternative ways to solve the problem.
3. Evaluation of the alternatives.
4. Making of the decision, either alone or in a team, based on the proposals made.
5. Implementation of the decision.
6. Evaluation of the decision, with the question if the problem is solved.

If we recall the PDCA cycle, we can classify the steps from one to four as *plan*. Step five is the *doing* phase and the sixth step is to be seen as *check*. Hence, what is missing is the *acting* phase, if necessary.

Let us have a look at how ResCoCo's specific situation could be applied to introduce an ethical sense into decision making while conducting a training session. First, what is the company's *problem*? The company has not been very successful in the past. The reason is that one of the corporate divisions is not profitable—most likely due to an outdated product range. Now it is the *aim* to ensure the company's survival. From a mere financial perspective, the easiest solution would be to dissolve the division. However, this would mean laying off employees. Another possibility to reduce costs would be to change the supplier of the main purchased good. But this probable supplier does obviously infringe human rights and pollute the environment. ResCoCo's challenge from a moral perspective, hence, is to ensure the company's survival, while, at the same time, not being complicit in human rights abuses and environmental pollution, and not laying off employees.

So, second, think of possible ways to *solve* the problem. Have you, for example, thought about talking to your existing supplier if you could find an agreement on lower prices? Maybe he is also interested in the survival of your company. Perhaps you would be able to find an investor if you changed your outdated product range—maybe toward sustainably friendly products. What else could you picture? Maybe there are also employees who want to bring new input toward sustainability and who are willing and able to dispense with parts of their salary for some time? Probably there are a lot more alternatives.

Third, ResCoCo's management and controlling would now need to *evaluate* the alternatives and to make the *decision*. We do not know how ResCoCo's management would decide. However, it is clear that decision making is much more difficult when taking into account other than monetary factors. So be prepared for that.

It is the target of this part of the training to achieve awareness and understanding that moral issues need to be integrated as a central point into *regular* decision making and must not be neglected. What we have not done so far is to set up a decision making guideline, which comprises both deontological ethics as a basis and KPIs for steering a company. This will be dealt with in Section 7.6 after we have further developed the fundamentals of responsible controlling. For these fundamentals, however, it is crucial to get a first understanding of responsibility within the proposed training.

6.6.3   *Creation of Awareness for Possible Dilemma Situations*

The first step in decision making is the definition of the problem. Already in this decision making step, most likely dilemmas will arise. For that reason, it is recommended that, within the training, dilemmas should be a separate part in order to make controllers aware of them. Subsequently, some alleged dilemmas are shown:

- Scarce resources in controlling versus triple bottom line measurement
- Shareholders versus other stakeholders
- Profit maximization versus morality

- Instrumental rationality versus ethical rationality
- Trade-offs between triple bottom line dimensions
- Trade-offs between today's and future generations.

In the following, I prototypically discuss these dilemmas to develop a sense for moral dilemmas in general.

The issue of scarce resources in controlling, can and must be solved by reallocating existing resources or by appointing new staff. Consequently, if no resources are established, your effort of installing controlling as a driver toward sustainability will fail right from the start. The question of shareholders versus other stakeholders or say profit maximization versus morality also looks like a moral dilemma. At this point, it is to discuss to whom a controller is responsible. It is to realize that a controller is an employee who has an employment contract and who has to bring a service to his employer.[25] Yet, that must not be a limitation for controllers when it comes to responsibility. A controller as a change agent must critically reflect the status quo. With respect to profits I come back to Ulrich. He states that profit is not to be condemned per se, but that it needs to be justified on the basis of legitimate grounds. Whether moral acting is appropriate or not against the backdrop of dispensing from profit can only be clarified by taking into account all legitimate claims[26]—the ones from the stakeholders as well as the claims from the shareholders. Yet, profit maximization versus morality represents a moral dilemma when taking into account different ethical perspectives—in this case, egoism or utilitarianism against ethics of rights and duties. Ulrich's two-tiered concept, however, overcomes this dilemma.

Also there could be the question of instrumental rationality in contrast to ethical rationality. An introduction is offered into the meaning of rationality, both in the responsibility and in the controlling section of this book. Ulrich argues that the core question of modern ethics

Think Outside the Box

- For whom is your organization doing what you are doing? Why?
- Which possible dilemma situations could occur in your organization when it comes to behaving more responsibly?

is to be seen in the *rational* justification of moral principles.[27] Thus, rational reflection is central to ethics. On the contrary, according to Weber and Schäffer, instrumental rationality as used in controlling only includes efficiency: resources need to be used in an efficient way in order to achieve given purposes or ends.[28] What seems to be a dilemma are just two parts of economic rationality, which must be combined in the sense of an integrative economic ethics.[29] The "problem of rational economic activity—. . . in an unabbreviated form— always basically comprises an ethical and a technical dimension."[30] The first one deals with "ethically rational (legitimate) purposes and principles of economic activity in view of possible alternative uses of limited resources."[31] The second one takes into account technical rationality— that is, efficiency—in order to achieve given purposes, but still under the "conditions of legitimacy."[32]

Ulrich admits that in today's neoclassical understanding, only instrumental rationality plays a role by asking *how* to economically manage the use of scarce resources. This represents, to put it in his words, "a concept of cost–benefit."[33] *For whom*, which means to what end the resources should be used is not reflected but seen as given, as also stated by Weber and Schäffer.[34] On basis of the elaborations concerning integrative economic ethics, we know that there are no ethically neutral spheres. Ethical rationality must not be neglected. Instead, the question *for whom* must always be considered if we recognize the unimpeachable human dignity. Hence, from an integrative economic ethics perspective, the contrast

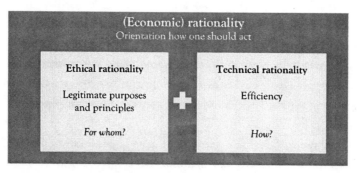

Figure 6.2 Unified conception of economic rationality

Source: On the basis of Ulrich, 2008a.

between instrumental rationality and ethical rationality is not to be questioned. This means there is no real dilemma situation. If we would take into account only one ethical perspective, like utilitarianism, we would end up with a dilemma situation. This is the reason why Ulrich argues for a two-tiered concept, which first considers deontological perspectives and later takes into account teleological factors.

Even though I follow an integrative ethical perspective and thus argue that morality is the basis for responsible controlling—instead of seeing profit maximization as an end in itself—there can also be other dilemmas. There could, for example, be trade-offs between the triple bottom line dimensions or between today's and future generations. One may raise the following exemplary questions: Is it better to invest in the establishment of a sound economic system in a Third World country, which feeds thousands of people today (intragenerational justice), even though it is evident that environmental problems arise? Or is it better to save the environment in order to enable future generations to fulfill their own needs (intergenerational justice)?

These exemplary dilemmas show that a responsible controller must be accustomed to the fact that there will not be a definite answer to many questions in the sense of right or wrong. Hence, decisions that are only made on the basis of hard facts will be the exception in responsible controlling. When asking how to deal with dilemmas, there is only one answer: by reflection and by acknowledging the unimpeachable freedom of every human being and its legitimate claims.

After having developed a general understanding of responsibility among controllers through training, an inherent nonconsequentialist ground for controlling behavior has to be defined as a next step.

Think Outside the Box

- Is your organization offering responsibility, sustainability, or ethics trainings? If not, how could you initiate that?
- How could you as a controller integrate ethical perspectives into the decision making process of your organization?

6.7   Step 7: Inherent Nonconsequentialist Ground for Controlling

Derived from the elaborations herein, I propose that we should take nonconsequentialist ethics into account to create a fundament for ethical conduct in controlling. We have elaborated that morality and thus the unimpeachable human freedom is to be taken into account when talking about nonconsequentialist ethics. It is the effort to establish a tangible responsible controlling framework. Therefore, I want to remind you again of the fundamental human rights and use them as a first layer of the responsible controlling framework. With this consideration, I link responsible controlling as well to the first two principles of the United Nations Global Compact, which state the following:

Principle 1: Businesses should support and respect the protection of internationally proclaimed human rights; and

Principle 2: make sure that they are not complicit in human rights abuses.[35]

We have to recognize that a controller may not be in a position to get a full overview of all human rights issues in which the organization is involved in general or in particular cases at hand. Yet, he or she can critically question the human rights issues and ask management to commission experts to find the answers. Remember ResCoCo's efforts.

After having established human rights as a fundament for controlling, I now add the duty ethics perspective. To do so, the second of Kant's maxims appears adequate for controlling. Even though there are many critics as stated earlier, with Kant's maxim we can reduce complexity for the controllers who are not experts in ethics. The second maxim—called human-end formula—is as follows:

Act in such a way as to treat humanity, whether in your own person or in that of anyone else, always as an end and never merely as a means.[36]

Persons, according to Kant, have intrinsic values that cannot be measured.[37] This view is a remarkable difference from a traditional controlling perspective. Nowadays, many companies' business aim—the alleged *end*—is the maximization of their profits. Hence, people are used as pure means. That is contradictory to Kant's categorical imperative. From a deontological ethical point of view, profit maximization can never be legitimized. Kant's

Dig Deeper

The United Nations Global Compact comprises ten principles within the following areas: human rights, labor, environment, and anticorruption.

If you want deeper insights, see the following website:

www.unglobalcompact.org/

categorical imperative can obviously serve as a situational independent, fundamental attitude of controlling behavior and, thus, represents a good reference point for responsible controlling. To avoid misunderstandings, it is important to note the following.

Kant's categorical imperative does not prohibit using people as means, what can be found in the expression "never merely as a means."[38] Otherwise, success-oriented action would always be reprehensible from a moral perspective. Our economy, based on the division of labor, would not work anymore. Yet, the boundary for that is the recognition of the unimpeachable human dignity, which must by no means be violated. It is only legitimized to use people as a means if they agree to that on basis of their unimpeachable freedom.[39] Remembering that ResCoCo should include its stakeholders into its decision making, treat them with respect, and not only make decisions about them. We look at the definition of stakeholders in Section 7.2.

Think Outside the Box

- Are you taking care of supporting and respecting human rights?
- What is the purpose or target of your organization?
- Do you have some behavioral guardrails in place that ensure that employees, customers, and all other stakeholders are always treated in a fair and legitimate manner?

To conclude this chapter, we can state the following **basis for responsible controlling**:

- No human right is violated.
- People are always treated as ends, and never only as a means.
- The controller himself is asked to imagine again and again what legitimate claims the stakeholders affected by a decision could have.

For all that, we need reflection of the status quo. Now the ethical basis of the controlling framework is set. In stage 1, we have had a look at soft factors and people. In stage 2, you will find hard factors and structures, which means I will give you even more tools at hand to implement responsible controlling.

CHAPTER 7

Stage 2: Hard Factors and Structures

"The things included in the measurement become relevant; the things omitted are out of sight and out of mind."[1]

—Peter Drucker

7.1 Step 8: Scope and Boundary for Responsible Controlling

Sustainability thinking means taking into account effects on the triple bottom line. I have argued that responsible controlling must meet this requirement and that it has to extend its scope from a mere financial perspective toward a holistic triple bottom line responsibility. Moreover, we have seen that (hyphenated) controlling is involved in nearly every corporate function when it comes to financial topics. However, with respect to responsibility, we need to clarify an important question at this point:

Are there organizational limits when it comes to controlling's responsibility?

The Global Reporting Initiative talks about *scope*, *boundary* and *time* when defining the report content.[2] Since I aim at integrating responsible controlling into existing approaches or deriving a method from them, I will take the two notions of *scope* and *boundary* in order to answer the question. *Scope* "refers to the range of sustainability Aspects covered in a report. The sum of the Aspects . . . reported should be sufficient to reflect significant economic, environmental and social impacts. It should also enable stakeholders to assess the organization's performance."[3] Thus, also for controlling like the one I aim at and that takes into account the triple bottom line, I define a limitation: we take into account the aspects that have significant impact. *Significant impact*, however, is not a clear-cut expression and thus remains, to a certain extent, a subjective judgment by the controller. To give orientation, I define the following:

> Responsible controlling acts within the scope of the triple bottom line and is committed to consider all significant issues. Above all, every aspect (without qualification) needs to be considered where human rights could be hurt.

Boundary, according to the Global Reporting Initiative, "refers to the description of *where* (italics added) impacts occur for each material Aspect. In setting the Aspect Boundaries, an organization should consider impacts *within and outside* (italics added) of the organization. Aspect Boundaries vary based on the Aspects reported."[4] Even though it is not my intention in this book to create a sustainability report, we observe that the mentioned boundaries from the Global Reporting Initiative are not strictly predefined. They vary from organization to organization. For some there may be more aspects with significant impacts outside the organization. For others the focus may lie internally.

Think Outside the Box

By asking sustainability questions when it comes to a purchase agreement, the awareness of sustainability topics is most likely moving to the purchaser and subsequently to the supplier. Sustainability topics, hence, leave your traditional finance and controlling area.

In addition, we cannot clearly define the boundary for responsible controlling. Yet, I argue for the following approach: if human rights are infringed, there is no valid organizational or operational boundary. Both company internal issues and issues at suppliers' or customers' sites are relevant. Controller's task is to always critically reflect whether human rights are respected. Controlling is in a good position to spread responsibility issues throughout the value chain.

Since it is my aim to introduce responsibility into every controlling function (purchasing-controlling, sales-controlling, and so on), the

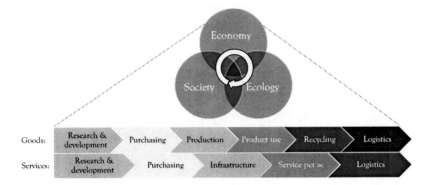

Figure 7.1 Scope and boundary of responsible controlling

Source: Adapted from Schulz (2012), p. 272, "Abb.1: "Triple-Bottom-Line" entlang der
Wertschöpfungskette" in A. Schneider, & R. Schmidpeter, Corporate Social Responsibility - Verantwortungsvolle Unternehmensführung in Theorie und Praxis. © Springer-Verlag Berlin Heidelberg 2012. With kind permission from Springer Science and Business Media.

boundary will automatically spread after every controller is aware of
responsibility topics.

Figure 7.1 shows how I summarize the scope and the boundary for
responsible controlling. The scope can generally be seen in every significant issue within the dimensions of the triple bottom line. As boundary
I do not set the financial consolidation boundary. Rather, internal and
external matters throughout the value chain must be considered. I extend
the boundary, ranging from suppliers to customers and from research and
development until the recycling stage.

Do you at this point see the link to the ResCoCo example? In
ResCoCo, human rights infringements are an issue. Both internal and
external issues are taken into account. Moreover, ResCoCo deals with
financial, social, and environmental issues. Moreover, it is the controller
who brings these topics onto the management agenda.

As a conclusion, we can state that there are no limits for controlling
when it comes to the responsibility of respecting humans as ends. You
need to ask critical questions whenever you think it is necessary. For all
other issues, controlling in practice could confine itself to issues with significant impact (that is, related to the notion of materiality, which we will
take up later on in the chapter).

Think Outside the Box

- What are the boundaries and scopes for your current controlling?
- How should boundaries and scopes be adapted for your future sustainability-oriented controlling?
- How would you convince your controlling coworkers that they should see the bigger picture and include responsibility topics within their day-to-day work?

7.2   Step 9: Consideration of Stakeholders

Currently, stakeholder thinking is not common in controlling. In the CSR and corporate sustainability area, however, it is one of the central aspects.

Within the context of Chapter 2 we have figured out that a stakeholder is every group or individual—living today or in the future—who has legitimate claims, regardless of whether the stakeholder has the power to really make the claim or not. Moreover, I have said that the basic principle in considering stakeholders must be seen in humans' morality and thus in the unimpeachable human dignity. In addition to this ideal of stakeholder identification, we have seen Mitchell, Agle, and Wood's approach of stakeholder prioritization, which is based on the three dimensions of *power*, *legitimacy*, and *urgency*.[5] In case a stakeholder can be classified into all three dimensions, he is a "highly salient stakeholder."[6] I agree to the fact that "what counts is not power, but good reasons."[7] Thus, *legitimacy* is acknowledged as the *ultimately decisive criterion* when it comes to stakeholder identification. Nevertheless, I consider Mitchell, Agle, and Wood's approach a good one to understand controlling's stakeholders. Thus far, stakeholder thinking is not prevalent in controlling. In the following I use the approach to (1) identify to whom mainstream controlling *does* ascribe importance to in reality and (2) which stakeholders *ought to* be considered. With respect to the latter (*ought to*), we notice that legitimacy must always be the basis regarding the question of who counts.

Regarding the first issue (to whom *is* importance ascribed?), it is to say that the major stakeholder of mainstream controllers is the manager. Controlling in the sense of steering a company is only possible through the interaction of managers and

> ## Think Outside the Box
>
> Which stakeholders could and should be taken into account when making corporate decisions? Management, and who else? Make a list!

controllers. The manager has power since he or she typically appoints the controller. Consequently, he or she has formal authority. Moreover, we can maintain that managers have urgent claims. It is controllers' task to support them in decision making, also in urgent ones. With respect to the third dimension—legitimacy—one can ask if managers' claims toward controllers are legitimate. Earlier, I have rejected Friedman's instrumental view that it is the only responsibility of managers "to make as much money for their stockholders as possible."[8] Instead, I have said that striving for profit must be grounded on legitimate claims. These claims, pursued by stockholders and managers, can only be justified if they do not infringe the unimpeachable human dignity, and thus if they do not treat profit itself as an end.

Thus, managers who would like to maximize profits would not be perceived as salient stakeholders, since they lack legitimacy. Yet, it is my aim to make an organization more responsible through controlling. On that ground alone—quite apart from the fact that a controller has a contractual duty to support management—we cannot and do not want to neglect management. Rather, responsible controlling must act to ensure that responsibility is recognized within management. Hence, management is and will remain a very important stakeholder—also in responsible controlling.

The second issue is a normative one: which stakeholders *ought to* be considered, beyond management? For answering this question, I recall Freeman again, who claims that a "stakeholder in an organization is . . . any group or individual who can affect or is affected by the achievement of the organization's objectives."[9] From an ethical perspective, it is important who *should* be able to raise legitimate claims,[10] and not who really has the power to influence organization's target achievement. Referring to Carroll's responsiveness dimension of the corporate social performance framework (see Chapter 4), I assign a proactive approach regarding social issues to responsible controlling. Therefore, subsequently, I broaden our perspective concerning stakeholders.

Think Outside the Box

Remember the reflection questions in Section 2.3? Have you really answered them? If not try to do now and make a stakeholder analysis of your current and future controlling and management accounting.

Especially when it comes to corporate decision making, not only management is a stakeholder. Hence, you need to identify further responsible controlling stakeholders based on power, urgency, and legitimacy—acknowledging that as soon as legitimacy is given, the stakeholder should be perceived as a salient one. To make Mitchell, Agle, and Wood's approach operationally useful for responsible controlling, I have developed a stakeholder identification table (Table 7.1). To identify and map controlling stakeholders, it is useful to think about them based on the view of different controlling institutions. By asking the sustainability controller and by including the respective functional controller (for instance, the sales controller) mentioning only the most obvious stakeholders, such as management, should be avoided. As can be seen in Table 7.1, responsible controlling, which supports management in its variety of tasks, is linked to a myriad of stakeholders. I also integrate *future generations* and the *ecosystem* as stakeholders, in order to take into account justice and the environmental part of the triple bottom line. Even though I consider three aspects—power, urgency, and legitimacy—legitimacy must always serve as the ground rule regarding the question of who counts. What do you think, how would the stakeholder identification table look like in ResCoCo's case? Management, employees, the current and possible future supplier, and the affected employees of the suppliers. Who else?

It is to mention that Table 7.1 makes no claim to be complete. Yet, it demonstrates a possibility for your controlling department to overcome its concentration on managers as the only stakeholders. Responsible controlling must broaden its view not only in terms of the triple bottom line but also with respect to legitimate stakeholders. For you as a controller

Table 7.1 Stakeholders of a responsible controlling

Stakeholders	Controlling function	Exemplary interconnection	Power		Urgency			Legitimacy
Managers	All	Every kind of decision making	Formal authority	x	Ad-hoc decisions	x	(x)	Dependent on profit approach
Shareholders	All	Striving for profit	Formal authority	x	Ad-hoc decisions	x	(x)	Dependent on profit approach
Employees	All	Good labor conditions vs. cost cuts	Influence on output; strike	x	Safety at work must be given	x	x	Must be paid and treated in a fair way
Customers	Sales	High quality vs. cheap products	Influence sales	x	Dependent on the issue at hand	(x)	x	Can expect non-harmful products
Suppliers	Purchasing	High quality vs. cheap products	Crucial for a functioning supply chain	x	Dependent on the issue at hand	(x)	x	Must be paid and treated in an adequate way
Competitors	All	Gaining each other's customers vs. job cuts at the respective sites	Potential to gain each other's customers	x	Dependent on the issue at hand	(x)	x	Competition must take place in a fair way
Governments	All	Regulation (e.g., prohibition of materials) vs. higher material cost	By law	x	Dependent on the issue at hand	(x)	x	Governments should act on behalf of human beings
Media / general public	All	Highly informative sustainability report vs. secret business information	Influence opinion and thus sales	x	Dependent on the issue at hand	(x)	(x)	Yes; given that media's claims are legitimate themselves
Neighborhood community	All	Job cuts vs. (instrumental) efficiency	Dependent on the issue at hand	(x)	Dependent on the issue at hand	(x)	x	Right to live an economically and ecologically sound life
Ecosystem	All	Environmentally friendly technologies vs. higher costs	Only through governments/ law	(x)	High, having in mind today's environmental condition	x	x	Ecosystems are the basis for human life
NGOs	All	Revelation of bad working conditions vs. higher labor costs	Dependent on the issue at hand	(x)	Dependent on the issue at hand	(x)	(x)	Yes; given that NGO's claims are legitimate themselves
Future generations	All	Keeping lives worth living in the long run vs. short term profit	Only through governments/ law	(x)	High, having in mind today's environmental condition	x	x	Unimpeachable human freedom

that could even mean being an advocate for somebody else than the manager and critically reflecting managers and stockholders attitudes, as well as their intended decisions. In this sense, controlling is not only a *business* partner but also a partner for *society* and the *environment*. After having identified general stakeholders of responsible controlling, I argue to establish an ongoing stakeholder dialog in order to (a) identify changing stakeholder claims on a regular basis and (b) put responsibility topics and a sense of urgency for them onto the agenda of (top) management, employees, and all other people involved.

7.3   Step 10: Target Contents, Materiality, and Adequate Key Performance Indicators

Think Outside the Box

Could you think of targets that could be applied within your organization to bring sustainability into your whole organization? Maybe it helps if you take a look again into Chapter 4 where I discussed KPIs. But do not forget to take into account the topics that are material!

The term *target* reminds us of the consequentialist ethics approach again. However, responsible controlling does not pursue an egoist or utilitarianist approach, like it could be the case in mainstream controlling. Instead, responsible controlling tries to take the foreseeable consequences of decisions and actions into account—also the nonfinancial ones. In addition to the deontological ground, it is meaningful to establish triple bottom line targets in an integrative way. This implies that the three dimensions of sustainabilty—ecology, economy, and society—must be understood as being tantamount. The reason why I heavily recommend establishing targets is that only KPIs are helpful for sustainable efforts that are linked to the responsibility of individuals.[11] To put it in another way, target setting is a crucial tool for us to bring responsibility into controllers', managers', and other employees' mindset. By breaking down the targets from top management to the employees, responsibility is becoming a topic throughout the whole organization.

7.3.1 Target Contents

When talking about targets, we should think about (1) the *target content* and (2) the *extent of targets*. In that order, please! Setting the *extent of targets* means, for example, to determine by how much percent the use of harzadous materials should decrease until a defined point of time. This is very important. But, before doing this the *target content, adequate KPIs*, and a *valid database* should be set up. For the purpose of defining the *content* of the targets themselves—for instance, should the reduction of hazardous materials be a key target for your organization at all?—I argue for a stakeholder-inclusive approach in order to figure out the issues with the highest priority. By including the stakeholders in defining the target content, we ensure that not only company's internal but also external factors, like human rights infringements, are taken into account. If your organization sees this stakeholder inclusion as a threat you may think about the positive effects of including stakeholders at such an early stage. You may get new ideas by listening to stakeholders—and even more important, you will reduce the risk of being accused for unethical behavior in the aftermath.

The database will be deliberately set up after having defined the target content. With this procedure, I recall Drucker's statement again. He claims that "the measurement (that means the indicator, which is) used determines to what one pays attention. It makes things visible and tangible. The things included in the measurement become relevant; the things

Think Outside the Box

- Go back to your stakeholder identification process (Section 7.2) and take the ones you identified as being the most important ones.
- How could you include them into the process of identifying target contents of your organization?
- What do you think: to what extent would your board let internal or external stakeholders have a say in target setting?
- Don't forget that this can be very valuable for your organization. Think about all the new ideas you might get by listening to stakeholders—and that is all for free!

omitted are out of sight and out of mind."[12] By listening to the stakeholders' opinion regarding material topics and including the stakeholders into the KPI-defining process, I want to avoid that things are out of mind which are relevant from a responsible point of view. The company on its own may not always be able to figure out all relevant factors—stakeholders can help with that.

Regarding the target content, from a practical standpoint, it is not appropriate in many cases to demand that controllers ask every possible stakeholder *personally* where he or she sees a need for action within the triple bottom line. Think about the time that would be needed for that. Rather, the controller must consider what *possible* legitimate interests and targets the identified salient stakeholders could have. Controlling should, hence, include these interests into the decision making process.

7.3.2 Materiality

Referring to the Global Reporting Initiative, I suggest making a materiality analysis in order to define the target contents. High materiality indicates that the content is of high importance and that there is a need to act. Contents of low materiality could rather be neglected. The Global Reporting Initiative sees aspects as material that have a high importance on two dimensions, which could be indicated in a matrix. On the one hand, these aspects are material that "reflect the organization's significant economic, environmental and social impacts"[13] and, on the other hand, those that would "substantively influence the assessments and decisions of stakeholders."[14]

I suggest a supplement to the two dimensions of the materiality matrix. After having defined the target content, it is important that the following questions regarding the intended *measures* are taken into account:

1. Is ethical rationality assured (*for whom is the issue relevant at all*)?
2. Is technical rationality assured (*how to treat the issue efficiently*)?

For responsible controlling, it is not enough to only answer the second question. If it is not clear for whom a measure could serve in a positive way at all, it is to question if your organization really should conduct it.

Think Outside the Box

Think of possible materiality topics in order to define your target contents. What is relevant for your organization and for its stakeholders?
   Is it...

Water scarcity	Fair competition	Diversity
Eco-efficiency	Trust	Abolition of child labor
Reduction of greenhouse gas emissions	Profitability	Transparency
Human rights	Product safety	Sustainability competence

.... or something totally different?

What do you think are material topics for ResCoCo's specific situation? Fair competition, fair treatment of the employees, appropriate return for shareholders or owners, fostering human rights, and accepting human dignity. And this list is not complete. The range of material topics is as diverse as the stakeholders of responsible controlling themselves. Furthermore, they highly depend on the type of organization. Hence, I abstain from listing a multitude of exemplary topics. Nevertheless, the following example makes it clear for you: if human rights infringements were identified as being probable or actually conducted by your organization or within its value chain, human rights would become definitely one content within the target system. Human rights, thus, would be a part of both the nonconsequentialist ground and the consequentialist target system of responsible controlling.

7.3.3   Key Performance Indicators

Although we have not established a database yet, as the next step after having identified the material issues, now adequate key performance indicators (KPIs) should be identified. Regarding the human rights example just made, we remember that one of the mentioned Global Reporting Initiative (GRI) indicators is concerned with the *total number and percentage of significant investment agreements and contracts that include human rights clauses or that underwent human rights screening.*[15] That, for instance, would be one valuable KPI for ResCoCo. I suggest taking the GRI as a first reference point when searching for adequate KPIs that are suitable for the defined target content. The environmental, social, and governance (ESG) approach largely driven by financial investors may be another option. However, GRI is more recognized in terms of stakeholder engagement. With respect to controlling itself, one content could be seen in making responsibility training for controllers. An appropriate KPI could be the *number of controllers who have undergone responsibility training*.

Think Outside the Box

Try to find suitable absolute and relative KPIs with which you can track and steer the material topics developed earlier.

We already know the absolute and relative KPIs. For controlling in the sense of steering an organization and helping in decision making, I argue for taking both absolute and relative KPIs into account when setting up targets. Absolute KPIs—for example, the total amount of accumulated waste water—provide information about the real impact on the world. Relative KPIs, on the other hand, may help a manager to steer his or her organization in a better way. This should be illustrated by using an example of two corporate entities, which could be compared with respect to the following KPI:

$$\frac{\text{total amount of accumlated waste water per entity}}{\text{number of employees working in the entity}}$$

If one entity is bigger than the other, it is comprehensible that *absolutely* more waste water is produced. In the example, I assume that also the *relative* consumption per employee is higher in the bigger entity. But why should the bigger one be allowed to use more waste water in *relation* to the number of employees? For controlling and management, the question that would arise is what is the smaller entity making differently and what can be learned out of that. As a target, the relative KPI of the bigger entity should decrease. Ceteris paribus, that would also affect the absolute waste water consumption of the company.

What is important to consider is the appropriateness of the KPIs with respect to steering the organization. External disclosure may have different requirements than controlling. I use GRI indicators as a helpful reference point. However, for a functioning controlling that is able to break down the responsibility targets and to derive measures, the targets have to be conveniently measurable. In practice, this depends on the type of organization, on the status quo of the controlling tools and methods and on the IT system you are using. That leads us to the next chapter, where we will have a look at the creation of an adequate data platform.

7.4   Step 11: Data Platform

Within the framework of this book we have elaborated that for responsible controlling not only measurable facts are important, but, first and foremost, it is the recognition of people as ends what constitutes the bedrock foundation of responsible controlling. Derived from that, we can state that not everything has to be measured exactly in responsible controlling. However, in order to establish a realistic controlling approach to be put into practice within your organization and to reach sustainability targets, the aspect of measurement must by no means be neglected. Therefore, an appropriate data platform must be set up—integrated in the financial platform, which most likely already exists in some way or other. Being clear about the material topics of your organization (which you have identified within the last chapter), for controlling now the question arises how to obtain the required information. *What* should be measured at all was clarified in the preceding step by doing the materiality analysis. Within this book, I focus on *how* to establish responsible controlling. Consequently, the issue arises *how* to implement a data platform that meets the requirements elaborated previously—especially those mentioned within the sufficiency analysis. The data platform needs to

a. bring transparency with regard to the triple bottom line;
b. provide internal and external data about material topics;
c. be integrated in existing systems;

d. ensure validity, reliability, objectivity, and efficiency;

e. encourage responsible decision making and allow the derivation of measures.

If we follow the suggestion to refer to the GRI, the points (a) and (b) are already resolved from a theoretical perspective. But, to turn an adequate data platform into practice, it must be convenient to set it up and maintain it. Moreover, just from a controlling capacity perspective, it will presumably not be possible to gather all necessary material data at once. Regarding (c) the integration of sustainability data into existing systems, Kiron et al. mention that "establishing data capture methods . . . and, more generally, making the transition to greater information transparency takes time."[16] I therefore argue for the following time-wise approach:

1. Definition, what data are needed (that point has already been discussed; see scope and boundary, stakeholders, target content, and materiality in Sections 7.1–7.3).
2. Check if data are already available in an existing information technology system within the company.
3. Check if data are already available in an existing information technology system outside the company, which can be used (such as accessible suppliers' data).
4. If not, creation of an adequate data source within the existing system by the responsibility controller, the respective controller (for instance, the purchasing-controller), and the respective specialist department.

Note that what you have just read within 30 seconds may take some months or longer within your organization. Make sure that you are provided (or if you are the manager: that you provide) enough time to execute these points and that you have a good team from all parts of the organization. For practical implementation, you find a checklist for setting up a data platform (Table 7.2).

Exemplarily for my proposed procedure, I illustrate that process for the social part of the triple bottom line—helping ResCoCo gathering data:[17]

Table 7.2 Checklist for setting up a data platform

	Question	Yes	No
Data needed	Have you defined scope and boundary of your responsible controlling realm? If not, have a look into Section 7.1.		
	Have you figured out which stakeholders should be taken into account in responsible decision making? If not, have a look into Section 7.2.		
	Have you defined what material target content is relevant and which KPIs could reflect them within your organization? If not, have a look into Section 7.3.		
	Have you set up the team you need to establish a triple bottom line data base (IT, logistics…)?		
Already available data within your organization	Have you checked with your controlling coworkers what data are available, for instance, in a business intelligence system?		
	Have you made appointments with every head of department to figure out if data are available which controlling does not know? (e.g., turnover rates in human resources department…)		
	Have you checked with your IT department what data are currently used in automated reports?		
	Have you checked with your IT department what data is available but is currently not used in automated reports?		
Already available data outside your organization	Has your purchasing department data from suppliers available? (e.g., ecological or social data)		
	Would your suppliers provide information about ecological or social data?		
	Have you asked them?		
	Have you thought about the way these data could be provided? (spreadsheets, IT-systems…)		
Creation of a new integrated data source	Have you checked which systems are currently used and which are the ones to be used? (spreadsheets, business intelligence software, enterprise resource planning software, clouds…)		
	Have you identified the persons and departments you need to have on board?		
	Have you agreed within the team with which material aspects you want to start? (emissions, human rights infringements…)		

First, the GRI indicators about labor practices and decent work[18] could be implemented, which are indicated as LA series in Figure 7.2. If controlling and human resources management collaborate, it is relatively easy to gather this information, because it should be available internally. Adequate Global Reporting Initiative KPIs could be the *type of injury and*

Figure 7.2 Order of implementing social sustainability metrics by difficulty level

rates of injury (to be found in indicator G4-LA6); G4-LA1, *total number and rates of new employee hires and employee turnover by age group, gender, and region*; and G4-LA9, *average hours of training per year per employee by gender, and by employee category*, which may include controllers' training itself. This category also includes G4-LA13 *ratio of basic salary and remuneration of women to men by employee category, by significant locations of operation*. This indicator could give a first glance about women's equality within your organization.

Having finished the (internal) LA series, in the next step an indicator of the society (SO) series could be implemented. G4-SO4, for example, includes the *total number and percentage of employees that the organization's anticorruption policies and procedures have been communicated to, broken down by employee category and region*. Gathering the number of this internally trained people is relatively easy.

Earlier, I have criticized that some persons hardly refer to any other criteria than the ones related to employees when it comes to social indicators[19] because they are easier to gather. Correspondingly, the human rights (HR[20]) series of the GRI is in my viewpoint the most difficult one to implement. G4-HR2—*total hours of employee training on human rights policies or procedures concerning aspects of human rights that are relevant to operations, including the percentage of employees trained*—is similar to G4-SO4 and still relatively easy to determine. G4-HR5, for example, *operations and suppliers identified as having significant risk for incidents of child labor, and measures taken to contribute to the effective abolition of child labor* is, from an ethical point of view, a very crucial indicator. However, this information cannot simply be gathered out of existing internal data systems. Measuring and reporting this indicator requires massive action in screening the suppliers and putting the information into the system. Screening the suppliers is not the task of the controller. Hence, close collaboration with the purchasing department is required.

It is to assume that suppliers would not provide information about, for example, child labor voluntarily for use within your system. More likely, they would do so in terms of waste water or emissions. At this point, it is to mention, that installing these KPIs is highly relevant for steering a company—but the installment process will take time and resources. You should be aware of that. Especially because of the fact that I assume human rights as being fundamental for responsible controlling I want to state the following.

Figure 7.2 must not be interpreted in a way that human rights indicators are the least important. Nevertheless, I deliberately show this order since a controller is accustomed to use internal systems. I assume that it is appropriate from an implementation viewpoint to start with information and issues a controller already knows (at least partly).

With respect to (d) that responsible controlling should ensure validity, reliability, efficiency, and objectivity, it is to say that the first three demand the same approach for responsible controlling than for a regular controlling. Objectivity, however, in responsible controlling does not only mean being objective on the basis of facts and figures on behalf of the manager, but trying to be a neutral agent of all legitimate stakeholders. Taking into account the triple bottom line approach supports that.

Think Outside the Box

Don't wait with bringing responsibility into your organization until experts provide you the perfect measurement and steering methods.

If you want to be a change agent and a good partner for management, think about unconventional approaches of bringing sustainability into managers' mindsets. Maybe the triple bottom line estimation approach can help you. And what else could help?

If your management board is business case driven, you may have a look at the sustainability advantage worksheets available here:[21]
www.sustainabilityadvantage.com/products/worksheets.html

The last claim regarding a good data platform was about encouraging responsible decision making and the facilitation of the derivation of measures (e). We have discussed that even though measuring CSR is difficult, it is crucial for managing and controlling responsibility. Moreover, we have figured out that not everything can be measured easily. Yet, from my standpoint, it would be reprehensible for controllers to wait until some experts develop an easily applicable impact analysis, which is also sufficient to steer an organization. Derived from that, I suggest an *additional*, unconventional controlling approach with respect to data. With this, I aim at introducing sustainability into the *mindsets* of management when making decisions, even though the data platform is still in the development stage. For this purpose I do not understand *data* in a sense that everything has to be measured accurately. Rather, I allow a data *estimation* as long as the data platform is not completely set up. In this endeavor, I refer to a concept that we already know.

With respect to the target of this book I aim at making an organization more responsible in a triple bottom line understanding. Earlier, we have said that sustainability is only given if all three dimensions of the triple bottom line are at least not negative. I therefore use Barbier's Venn diagram, but take numerical indexes (Figure 7.3). Only if a *four* is estimated within all three dimensions we expect a decision to have a positive or at least no negative impact onto the triple bottom line. If you sum it up for the issue you are looking at and you are sure every aspect would at least not be negatively influenced, you would then count a value of 12. If in another issue, impacts on society and economy would both be assigned a four—meaning that it is a good project regarding these

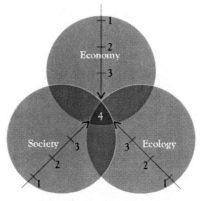

Figure 7.3 Triple bottom line estimation

views—and ecology would only get a one, the issue or project would have a sum of nine and would thus not be sustainable. How would it look in the ResCoCo case? Let us assume the management board tends to close the division that is currently not profitable. From an ecology perspective, this would probably be good, since fewer products are manufactured. So we assume a three. Regarding the economic side, we take a narrow view and only regard ResCoCo itself. Here, we assign a four since it helps the company to survive. At the societal part of the triple bottom line we allocate a one, after all we had to lay off employees. In sum, we count eight points for this decision. Now think about other possible decisions! To what would you sum them up? And which decision would you suggest?

I see a big advantage in the use of the *triple bottom line estimation*. Even though the data may not be accurate enough for external reporting, the estimation keeps triple bottom line aspects in managers' and controllers' mind. Controlling, as we have learned, must not provide accurate figures in all cases but must support management decision making. In terms of responsibility, it must extend its focus from only being monetary driven toward the triple bottom line. Earlier, I have maintained that controllers should be change agents. With this approach we go a step toward that claim, by encouraging responsible decision making and by allowing the estimation of effects.

> ### Think Outside the Box
>
> Think of projects and issues in the past! Where could you have used the triple bottom line estimation in order to make sustainability a topic in corporate decision making?
>
> Where could you use this tool or others in the future?

7.5 Step 12: Fostering Responsibility Through Communication

When it comes to encouraging people toward responsibility, communication is very important. The last step of the responsible controlling roadmap therefore deals with *communication*. How the required information can be gathered is of importance for a helpful controlling function. In addition, an adequate method of disseminating the acquired information in order to support management in responsible decision making needs to be established. Earlier, we had a look at the GRI and at the environmental, social, and governance indicators. Within the framework of this book, the focus is on controlling and managing an organization. External reporting may be a first reference point with respect to KPIs, but it is not enough when it comes to steering a company. In responsible controlling, it is not sufficient to report once a year. The report frequency must be adapted to stakeholders' needs. This means, it must be adequate to the demands of both managers and other stakeholders. Regarding managers, it is to say that they must get information when they have to make decisions. All other stakeholders should be able to access information about the progress of measures on a regular basis. I argue for the following approach, which I perceive as being realistic with respect to controlling's resources:

First, use existing management reports! Ecological and social KPIs should be integrated into existing internal management reports. With that, you ensure that managers do not have to become accustomed to a new report since they find sustainability information within a familiar layout. At ResCoCo, the controller and the management board decided to integrate the *total hours of employee training on human rights policies* into the existing management report. As a consequence, responsible information is being kept in managers' minds on a regular basis. In addition, investors may find sustainability information in the reports you send them. With respect to information for decision making, I propose taking the triple bottom line estimation graph (Figure 7.3) into account.

Second, keep your employees updated on a regular basis to ensure that they are aware of responsibility topics! Schulz argues that it is important to

Think Outside the Box

Report in pictures:

What do you think is easier to understand for many people:

"We have saved an amount of waste water of 150,000 liter."

or

"We have saved an amount of waste water that is roughly equivalent to 1,000 full bathtubs"?

Probably it is the mixture of both statements which makes the information clear!

get employees emotionally involved.[22] Therefore, I propose to *translate* sustainability figures for employees. Tons of saved CO_2 emissions could, for instance, be shown by using the number of cars that emit the same amount of emissions. Cases of human rights infringements should not only be demonstrated by a pure number, but in addition, drawings (not photographs) of harmed people should be illustrated within the reporting. With such *translation*, emotional involvement and awareness of employees is probably going to rise. An adequate awareness raising reporting equipment toward employees could be a monitor at a central place within the company, for example, at the entrance of the cafeteria. This monitor should show regular updates of the just-mentioned *translated* KPIs. Also the screen saver of your computers could be used to show, for example, the amount of used electricity of the respective department with a comparison to the average usage of all departments. Show sustainability data at as many places as possible.

Third, let all other stakeholders know regularly how you proceed with your sustainability efforts! With respect to these stakeholders, it is imaginable to report on the Internet—for example, by using the GRI indicators, and also by *translating* the issues into figures and drawings.

In conclusion, communication with respect to responsible controlling does not aim at taking over the task of corporate communications by creating glossy brochures. Rather, it is the aim of fostering responsibility by disseminating awareness throughout the organization. To achieve that, the integration into existing reports and the *translation* for employees is perceived as being practicable from a controlling point of view. If business intelligence systems are already available within your organization, this may help you a lot at this stage. Regarding external reporting, your corporate communications department may be a valuable partner for you.

Think Outside the Box

Which existing reports could you use to include sustainability data and to disseminate them easily?

Think about measures in order to make your employees emotionally involved? Show not only "boring" figures but also tell stories!

How would you inform external stakeholders?

One very important point in communication with respect to responsible controlling has not been targeted so far: what happens if you as a controller realize the importance of sustainability and you want to become active, your management board, however, is not interested in these topics? In other words, *how to get top-management commitment and how to avoid pushback from management?* First of all, do not behave like a moralizer. Rather, try to convince your board with the following arguments:

- You understand the core processes of the organization. And you realized that there is a lot of potential, both regarding ecological and social topics (for example, less environmental pollution and better employee satisfaction) and regarding the possibility to improve the financial bottom line (for instance, by improving energy efficiency).

- You have an awareness of the raising problems in this world and a sense of urgency for them. Make clear that dealing with sustainability topics may be crucial for the long-term survival of the organization. After all, there is an increasing public awareness for sustainability.

- You have an idea how to close the gap between the desired state of a sustainable company and the actual state. Here you can bring first examplary KPIs into play. Furthermore, stress that innovations never came from backward thinking.

- You have or you are willing to achieve knowledge about sustainability tools, like the triple bottom line estimation and stakeholder analyses. The same applies to ethical thinking.

- And show first quick gains, even if small ones. For instance, reduction of both paper usage and costs by implementing double-sided printing. This indicates your willingness to act toward a more responsible company.

- However, do not forget that it is not the sole business case that responsible controlling wants to pursue. Also let your board know that taking over responsibility is one of the basic principles of interacting with stakeholders.

- All in all, show that sustainable behavior is not a threat but a major and holistic opportunity for your organization that can improve all three parts of the triple bottom line.

The fact that the threat of management pushback is coming at this stage of the book is no coincidence. I believe that the insights, concepts, and argumentations you have found so far will help you to better argue for a responsible behavior and to convince your management board.

Up until now, you have found 12 steps how responsible controlling can be implemented within your organization. From a practical viewpoint, it is crucially necessary to allocate resources. Responsible controlling is based on a nonconsequentialist ground but is extended by a consequentialist target approach. With that, I am confident that an applicable responsible controlling framework can be integrated into your organization. As a last step (not belonging to the roadmap anymore), I show how everything I have developed so far could be wrapped up and be merged into the decision making process of your organization.

7.6   Wrapping Up Responsible Controlling and Merging it in the Decision Making Process

Within 12 steps we have elaborated (a) what I understand as an ethical ground for controlling, (b) what could be suitable KPIs in terms of responsibility, and (c) how we could define and implement them. Moreover, we have discussed (d) the scope of responsible controlling and (e) how we can identify our stakeholders. Now, after having finished the elaborations of the steps of implementing a responsible controlling framework, I will set up a tool for supporting your decision making on a responsible ground. I will do so by synthesizing the developed aspects.

Earlier, I have stated that a controller may not be an ethics expert. Hence, in order to make him a *responsible* controller despite this fact, I will use a questionnaire for responsible decision making that aims at merging deontology, with its generalizable principles, and teleology with its targets. The questionnaire—shown in Table 7.3—is based on the steps of the PDCA cycle.

Table 7.3 *Responsible controlling cycle in decision making*

PDCA	Context	Questions
Plan	General	Is it a material issue at all?
		Have moral issues been identified? If yes, which ones?
	Targets	What are the targets of the intended actions?
		Does the intended action contribute to our superior objective of making the organization more responsible? (positive or at least no negative effect onto the triple bottom line)
		How does the status quo and the desired state look like within the triple bottom line estimation?
		Are the targets only instrumental (e.g., profit maximization)? --> reject intended action
		Have adequate sustainability KPIs been identified in order to track target achievement?
		What are foreseeable consequences (not necessarily intended ones) of the decision?
	Responsible ground	Have we acknowledged the unimpeachable human dignity, that is, are people being perceived as ends (human end formula)? If not --> reject intended action
		Is it probable that the intended action infringes human rights?
		Which stakeholders could have legitimate claims regarding the action and the consequences?
		Are we involving the legitimate stakeholders in the ongoing decision making process? --> decision taking together with those affected
		How would the stakeholders argue?
		Have we taken into account both ethical and technical rationality?
		Have we critically reflected the decision and searched for alternatives?
		Is the decision appropriate with respect to all legitimate stakeholders (also with respect to shareholders)?
		Have we already communicated the decision, before implementing it?
Do	—	Implementation of the decision
Check	Targets and responsible ground	Ask questions from *plan* again
		Plan–actual comparison: What do the KPIs tell us about our triple bottom line performance?
		Do we need to change the targets (feedforward) or the intended actions (feedback)? --> If yes: how?
		Morality check: Have there been (other than expected) moral issues? Why? Which ones?
Act	—	Establish corrective measures if necessary

How would ResCoCo's controller probably answer these questions in regard to the decisions she or he must prepare for her or his management board? As you already know at this point, there is often no clear-cut right or wrong with respect to decisions in the realm of corporate sustainability. However, there are better or worse decisions! The shown questionnaire illustrates a tool for responsible controlling, which keeps responsibility in the mind of both controllers and all other people involved. Earlier, I have asked the question how sustainability awareness can be broken down and integrated into the different corporate functions. Now I can answer:

An awareness for responsibility and sustainability can be disseminated within your organization by making the responsible controlling questionnaire a compulsory step before approving decisions. Then controlling is able to integrate responsible topics cross-departmental in every corporate function and on all corporate levels. Hence, controlling can become a driver and a change agent and can develop a positively fostering influence on sustainability.

CHAPTER 8

Summing It All Up

"Controlling, like the combustion engine, is a mature technology that you should now reinvent in order to make your organization a pioneer for a responsible and sustainable age."[1]
—Daniel Ette, referring to Gary Hamel

You may remember that initially I have shown that controlling departments are hardly involved in sustainability topics. They do not contribute to corporate responsibility. On this basis, it was the aim to reinvent controlling in such a way that it can become a driver toward sustainability. Now it is up to you to put all we have elaborated within the previous chapters into your organizational practice! To make the concept of responsible controlling ultimately clear for you, I am going to sum everything up now.

As a foundation for the effort, I have thoroughly examined the notion of *responsibility* within Chapter 2 by having had a look at ethical aspects. We have found out that *morality* and thus the unimpeachable freedom of all human beings is a cornerstone when it comes to responsibility. Moreover, instead of taking one ethical approach into account we have seen that it is valuable to look through a "prism" of ethical theories in order to understand the full picture of the issue.

Within Chapter 3, I have introduced the term *controlling*. I have shown what is to be understood by controlling in an organizational context and in which areas controllers are active. Afterward, we have regarded different controlling approaches toward sustainability (Chapter 4). This has led to the realization that the prevalent controlling concepts are not sufficient with respect to responsibility but that they indicate a valuable basis on which we could build a synthesized approach.

Through the development of a responsible controlling roadmap in Chapters 5, 6, and 7, I have given recommendations *how* the status quo of controlling should be altered in terms of both tools and mindsets. I have elaborated how controlling can contribute to foster a corporation's responsible behavior and how sustainability topics can be integrated in management decisions. With regard to decisions, I have exposed that the basis for *good* decisions is to be seen in the recognition of all legitimate claims and thus in the unimpeachable human dignity of all human beings. However, I have not provided a catalog with clear-cut answers or behavioral instructions. On the contrary, it has become evident that ethics as a *critical reflection* effort is central to responsible controlling. That is why you have found many reflection boxes within this book. Decisions in a responsible sense will not be made on hard facts, like profit, as the sole criterion. In addition, soft facts must be reflected according to the motto "legitimacy has priority over success."[2] Within the context of an integrative economic ethics I have shown that ethics must not be seen as a restriction to profit, but that it should constitute the fundament for all economic behavior—also for controlling and management accounting within your organization. The saying, "if you can't measure it, you can't manage it"[3] is only partly true for responsible controlling. Even though I have acknowledged the importance of key performance indicators and of a valid database, I have shown that "human beings are at the centre of concerns for sustainable development"[4] and thus for responsible controlling—and for you!

My assertion from the beginning was the following:

> **Responsible controlling is indispensable to make an organization more responsible.**

To defend that, I now have a look at the sufficiency analysis again. Controlling as a support function for management plays an indispensable cross-departmental role when it comes to the question how an organization can become more responsible. As long as controlling acts in an instrumental, profit-maximizing way, it will be difficult to establish responsibility within all realms of a corporation. Therefore, **it is indispensable to make controlling itself responsible if corporate responsibility should be assumed.** By further developing the existing methodological competences of controllers and by bringing an ethical understanding into their minds—as I have done it within this book—I can ensure that responsibility can be spread throughout the organization. With the responsible controlling roadmap I have developed a tool that contributes a lot to controlling's *responsible development.* I strongly hope that you have the chance and the capability to introduce responsible controlling within your organization.

The different steps of the roadmap give recommendations and show tools how responsibility can be transferred into controlling practice. Responsible controlling must be based on a nonconsequentialist ground. In addition, adequate sustainability targets must be measured and set up. Stakeholder thinking is important for responsible controlling. The main criterion for stakeholder identification and prioritization is the legitimacy of their claims—not to be confused with mere power. I have established the framework as a holistic approach. Both intergenerational and intra-generational justice are taken into account, as well as aspects throughout the value chain. Important to note is that I have extended the focus of controlling from a financial perspective toward a triple bottom line understanding.

I do not picture responsible controlling as a straight road. I rather see it as a cycle. Also for the responsible controlling concept, the PDCA cycle is valuable. What I have done within this book is *planning.* Now it is up to you! Start the doing phase of implementing the framework into your day-to-day practice! After that I suggest you make a check again. If necessary, the roadmap should be revised and corrective actions should be executed. Responsible controlling ought to be understood as a continuous improvement process. Similar to what Schneider says about CSR.[5] At this point, I invite every reader of this book to join the discussion about the implementation of a responsible controlling. Please let me know what your experiences are when it comes to controlling, responsibility and sustainability. Hopefully, with these hints the concept can be developed even further. My email address can be found at the end of the text.

Table 8.1 links the steps of the responsible controlling roadmap and the attributes that we have assigned to responsible controlling. It should help you to get a final clear picture.

Table 8.1 Concluding analysis of responsible controlling approach

Criteria for responsible controlling		Tool / step within roadmap
Ethical approach	Consequentialist	Step 10: Definition of target contents and adequate key performance indicators (Section 7.3)
	Nonconsequentialist	Step 7: Definition of an inherent nonconsequentialist ground for controlling (Section 6.7)
Target	Profit maximization	-----
	Based on morality	Step 6: Development of a responsibility understanding through training (Section 6.6)
Stakeholder approach	Based on acceptance	-----
	Based on legitimacy	Step 6: Development of a responsibility understanding through training (Section 6.6)
Justice	Intergenerational	Step 6: Development of a responsibility understanding through training (Section 6.6)
	Intragenerational	
Holistic approach	Internal	
	External (including supply chain)	Step 8: Scope and boundary for a responsible controlling (Section 7.1)
Focus and transparency on triple bottom line	Ecology	
	Economy	
	Society	
Relevance for steering a corporation	KPIs and KPI-system	Step 10: Definition of target contents and adequate key performance indicators (Section 7.3); Step 11: Data platform (Section 7.4)
	Support for decision making	All Steps; responsible controlling cycle in the decision making process (Section 7.6)
	Derivation of measures	All Steps; responsible controlling cycle in the decision making process (Section 7.6)
Integration	... in existing systems	Step 11: Data platform (Section 7.4)
	... in core business processes and strategy	All steps; Above all: Step 4: Definition of a vision and creation of a controlling mission statement (Section 6.4); Step 5: Definition of a strategy (Section 6.5)
Controlling as change maker	Critical reflection of actual controlling behavior	Step 3: Analysis of the status quo (Section 6.3)

Finally, I would like to take a look into the future. Most likely, it will not be an easy task to integrate ethical thinking into actual controlling behavior and to make responsibility a cornerstone of controlling. One crucial element will be the fact that in the current economic scenario, instrumentalist thinking is still prevalent. It is to avoid a situation in which companies that behave responsibly are the losers in the market since they have to compete with rivals that do not take morality as a basis for their actions. Ulrich, therefore, claims the necessity of a "supranational framework of global competition."[6] In the same direction, it can be reasoned that "a combination of legitimizing pressures from civil society . . . and a . . . legally binding global regulatory framework" is needed.[7] However, the missing regulatory framework should not be an excuse for irresponsible organizational and personal comportment. I am convinced that responsible controlling as a *critical reflection* effort can and must contribute a lot to foster an organization's responsible behavior. Therefore, responsible controlling must first and foremost be understood as a mindset.

If controllers realize that "not everything that can be counted counts and not everything that counts can be counted,"[8] if they change both their mindsets and their tools toward responsibility and if they encourage others to do so as well, they can push responsibility into the whole organization. Thus, I can claim as a conclusion:

Responsible controlling is an uncommon but indispensable approach of making an organization more responsible.

About the Author

Daniel A. Ette is energy and climate protection manager in a German medium-sized company and consultant for sustainability controlling and sustainable corporate management. In the past years, he worked as CSR consultant in a European Union project for implementing corporate responsibility in small- and medium-sized enterprises. Before that Mr. Ette implemented a sustainability controlling system for an international company. In 2012, his efforts were honored when the company he worked for was rewarded for Mr. Ette's innovations with the "green controlling" award of the Péter Horváth foundation—one of the leading controlling think tanks in Europe.

In addition, Mr. Ette is a lecturer at different universities. Among others, he teaches corporate responsibility at the excellence university of Constance in Germany, and values in business at the Baden-Wuerttemberg Cooperative State University. Furthermore, he was part of the working group green controlling of the International Controllers Association which published a book on green controlling. Mr. Ette has a German diploma in business economics and a master of arts in Responsible Management. In order to contact him please use the following e-mail address: daniel.ette@responsible-controlling.com

Notes

Chapter 1

1. Wilde (2009), p. 100.
2. Lubin and Esty (2010).
3. Lubin and Esty (2010).
4. Lubin and Esty (2010), p. 50.
5. van Marrewijk (2003).
6. Friedman (1970).
7. Smith and Playfair (1811).
8. Jorberg (2010).
9. Gastinger and Gaggl (2012).
10. United Nations (2010, 2011).
11. KPMG (2012).
12. Kiron, Kruschwitz, Haanaes, and von Streng Velken (2012).
13. Lotter and Braun (2010).
14. Weber, Georg, Janke, and Mack (2012).
15. United Nations (2000).
16. Ernst and Young (2012).
17. Schaltegger, Windolph, and Harms (2010).
18. Wilde (2009), p. 100.
19. Meadows, Meadows, Zahn, and Milling (1972).
20. Stabenow (2010).
21. Schaltegger, Windolph, and Harms (2010).
22. Schaltegger, Windolph, and Harms (2010).
23. Schaltegger, Windolph, and Harms (2010).
24. Crane and Matten (2010), p. 5.

Chapter 2

1. John D. Rockefeller, Jr., as cited in Maxwell (2003), p. 132.
2. Oxford University Press (2012b).
3. Oxford University Press (2012b).
4. Oxford University Press (2012b).
5. Oxford University Press (2012b).
6. Suchanek (2012).
7. Within this book we use the terms *organization, corporation, company,* and *firm* as synonyms.

8. Suchanek (2012).
9. Suchanek (2012).
10. Carroll (1979), p. 500.
11. Commission of the European Communities (2001), p. 6.
12. Oxford University Press (2012a).
13. European Commission (2011), p. 3.
14. Carroll (1979).
15. European Commission (2011), p. 6.
16. European Commission (2011), p. 6.
17. European Commission (2011).
18. International Organization for Standardization (2010).
19. International Organization for Standardization (2010), Introduction.
20. International Organization for Standardization (2010), sec. 2.18.
21. International Organization for Standardization (2010), sec. 2.18.
22. International Organization for Standardization (2010).
23. Garriga and Melé (2004).
24. Crane and Matten (2010), p. 57.
25. Schneider (2012).
26. Schneider (2012), p. 19.
27. Schneider (2012).
28. International Organization for Standardization (2010), Introduction.
29. Carlowitz (2009).
30. Carlowitz (2009).
31. United Nations (1987).
32. United Nations (1987).
33. United Nations (1987).
34. United Nations (1992).
35. Carlowitz spoke about *Nachhaltigkeit*, which is the German word for sustainability.
36. Russ (2010), p. 61.
37. Elkington (1998).
38. Cambridge University Press (2014).
39. Cambridge University Press (2014).
40. Elkington (1998).
41. Kuhn (2008).
42. Savitz and Weber (2006), p. xiii.
43. Kuhn (2008).
44. Bachmann (2011).
45. Barbier (1987).
46. Pezzey (1997), p. 448.
47. Friedman (1970), p. 6.

48. Friedman (1970).
49. Friedman (1970), p. 5.
50. Garriga and Melé (2004).
51. Garriga and Melé (2004), p. 53.
52. Tschandl (2012).
53. Crane and Matten (2010).
54. Oxford University Press (2013).
55. Willard (2012).
56. Vaude (2013).
57. David (2013).
58. BP (2012), p. 16.
59. Schreck (2012).
60. International Organization for Standardization (2010), sec. 2.18.
61. Garriga and Melé (2004), p. 60.
62. Fenner (2008).
63. Thielemann (2010).
64. Crane and Matten (2010), p. 5.
65. Crane and Matten (2010), p. 5.
66. Within the framework of this book, we look at corporations that means at businesses. Businesses act in a global economy. Due to that reason and for simplicity reasons I do not distinguish deliberately between business ethics and economic ethics.
67. Ulrich (2008b).
68. Ulrich (2008b).
69. Ulrich (2008a), p. 86.
70. Ulrich (2008a), p. 101.
71. Ulrich (2008a).
72. Ulrich (2008a).
73. Ulrich (2008a).
74. Within the further course of this book, I will use the adjective "moral" in the sense of the noun "morality" and not referring to the noun "moral."
75. International Organization for Standardization (2010), sec. 2.18.
76. Carroll (1979), p. 500.
77. Ulrich (2008a).
78. Thielemann & Wettstein (2008), p. 8.
79. Crane and Matten (2010).
80. Crane and Matten (2010), p. 98.
81. Crane and Matten (2010), p. 100.
82. Crane and Matten (2010).
83. Crane and Matten (2010).
84. Crane and Matten (2010), p. 101.

85. Mandal (2010), p. 44.

86. Crane and Matten (2010), p. 102.

87. Fenner (2008).

88. United Nations (2012).

89. Ruggie (2008), p. 16.

90. United Nations (2012).

91. Thielemann (2010).

92. Kant (1785), p. 29.

93. Thielemann (2010).

94. Kant (1785), p. 33.

95. Fenner (2008).

96. Crane and Matten (2010), p. 93.

97. Crane and Matten (2010), p. 94.

98. Crane and Matten (2010), p. 128.

99. Crane and Matten (2010), p. 128.

100. Economy for the Common Good (2013).

101. Alternative Bank Switzerland (2014).

102. Crane and Matten (2010), p. 5.

103. John D. Rockefeller Jr., as cited in Maxwell (2003), p. 132.

104. Carroll (1979), p. 500.

105. Carroll (1979).

106. Carroll (2004), p. 117.

107. Carroll (1979), p. 500.

108. Carroll (2004).

109. Crane and Matten (2010).

110. Carroll (2004).

111. Handelsgesetzbuch (2005), Article 289 (3).

112. Carroll (1979), p. 500.

113. Carroll (1979).

114. Carroll (1979), p. 500.

115. Crane and Matten, (2010), p. 54.

116. Carroll (1979).

117. Carroll (1979).

118. Carroll (2004).

119. Carroll (1979).

120. Jasch (2012).

121. Friedman (1962), p. 133.

122. Freeman (1984), p. 46.

123. Crane and Matten (2010), p. 62.

124. Evan and Freeman (1993).

125. Mitchell, Agle, and Wood (1997).

126. Mitchell, Agle, and Wood (1997), p. 853.
127. Mitchell, Agle, and Wood (1997), p. 853.
128. Mitchell, Agle, and Wood (1997), p. 853.
129. Mitchell, Agle, and Wood (1997), p. 853.
130. Thielemann and Wettstein (2008).
131. Thielemann and Wettstein (2008), pp. 31–32.
132. Englisch, Sahr, Volkmann, Blank, and Tokarski (2012).
133. Englisch, Sahr, Volkmann, Blank, and Tokarski (2012).
134. Schaltegger, Windolph, and Harms (2010).
135. Thielemann and Wettstein (2008), p. 29.
136. Thielemann and Wettstein (2008), p. 31.
137. Thielemann and Wettstein (2008), p. 31.
138. Thielemann and Wettstein (2008), p. 36.
139. Mitchell, Agle, and Wood (1997).
140. Mitchell, Agle, and Wood (1997), p. 873.
141. Mitchell, Agle, and Wood (1997).
142. Thielemann and Wettstein (2008), p. 32.
143. Thielemann and Wettstein (2008), p. 37.
144. Goodpaster (1991), p. 57.
145. Ulrich (2008a).
146. Ulrich (2008a).

Chapter 3

1. Albert Einstein, as cited in Everett, Johnson, and Madden (2012).
2. Eschenbach and Siller (2009).
3. Anthony (1965), p. 28.
4. Eschenbach and Siller (2009).
5. Albert Einstein, as cited in Everett, Johnson, and Madden (2012).
6. Eschenbach and Siller (2009).
7. Institute of Management Accountants (2012).
8. Beckers (2010).
9. Ziegenbein (2007), p. 25; translated.
10. Wöhe and Döring (2010), p. 189; translated.
11. Weber and Schäffer (2000).
12. Weber and Schäffer (2000).
13. Horváth (2006).
14. Weissmann (2005).
15. Gutenberg (1958).
16. Weissmann (2005).
17. International Group of Controlling (2013).

18. International Group of Controlling (2013).
19. in German: Internationaler Controller Verein; ICV.
20. Internationaler Controller Verein e.V. (2002).
21. Internationaler Controller Verein e.V. (2002).
22. Internationaler Controller Verein e.V. (2002), p. 5; translated.
23. Weissmann (2005).
24. Ziegenbein (2007).
25. as cited in Baier (2008), p. 19.
26. Baier (2008).
27. Baier (2008).
28. Mund (2009).
29. Buchholz (2009).
30. Buchholz (2009).
31. Rickards (2007).
32. Preißler (2007).
33. Eschenbach and Siller (2009).
34. Gälweiler (2005).
35. Buchholz (2009).
36. Preißler (2007).
37. Buchholz (2009).
38. Eschenbach and Siller (2009).
39. Eschenbach and Siller (2009).
40. Buchholz (2009).
41. Drucker (2012).
42. Eschenbach and Siller (2009).
43. Schäffer and Weber (2005).
44. Tschandl (2012).
45. Eschenbach and Siller (2009).
46. Mutafelija and Stromberg (2003).
47. Mutafelija and Stromberg (2003).
48. Eschenbach and Siller (2009).
49. Buchholz (2009), p. 34.
50. Buchholz (2009).
51. International Group of Controlling (2012).
52. International Group of Controlling (2012).
53. International Group of Controlling (2012).
54. Eschenbach and Siller (2009).
55. Gladen (2011).
56. Gladen (2011).
57. Buchholz (2009).
58. Eschenbach and Siller (2009).

59. Buchholz (2009).
60. Eschenbach and Siller (2009).
61. Eschenbach and Siller (2009).
62. Buchholz (2009).
63. Eschenbach and Siller (2009).
64. Weissmann (2005).
65. Eschenbach and Siller (2009).
66. Eschenbach and Siller (2009).
67. Buchholz (2009).
68. CONTROLLING-Portal.de (2014).
69. Kaplan and Norton (1996), p. 21.
70. Drucker (2007), p. 56.

Chapter 4

1. Raghubir, Roberts, Lemon, and Winer (2010), p. 69 taking a study of Margolis, Elfenbein, and Walsh (2007) into account.
2. Ries and Wehrum (2011).
3. Ries and Wehrum (2011).
4. Schaltegger, Windolph, and Harms (2010).
5. Schaltegger, Windolph, and Harms (2010).
6. Reichmann and Kißler (2010).
7. Reichmann and Kißler (2010), p. 106.
8. Ries and Wehrum (2011).
9. Schaltegger, Windolph, and Harms (2010).
10. Internationaler Controller Verein (2010).
11. Tschandl and Posch (2012).
12. Tschandl and Posch (2012).
13. Horváth, Isensee, and Michel (2012).
14. Internationaler Controller Verein (2014).
15. Hemel (2011).
16. Müller (2011).
17. Günther and Stechemesser (2011).
18. Kersten, Becker, Allonas, and Berlin (2011).
19. Internationaler Controller Verein (2011).
20. Internationaler Controller Verein (2011)
21. Internationaler Controller Verein (2011).
22. Internationaler Controller Verein (2011).
23. Internationaler Controller Verein (2011).
24. Internationaler Controller Verein (2011).
25. Günther and Stechemesser (2011), p. 418.

26. Günther and Stechemesser (2011).
27. Michel (2011).
28. Günther and Stechemesser (2011).
29. Günther and Stechemesser (2011), p. 442.
30. Günther and Stechemesser (2011), p. 442.
31. Günther and Stechemesser (2011).
32. Michel (2011).
33. Published in German under the title *Nachhaltigkeitscontrolling*.
34. Deutsch, Krüger, and Michel (2012).
35. Prengel (2012).
36. Müller (2012).
37. Müller (2012).
38. Müller (2012), p. 83.
39. Ramanathan (1976).
40. Ramanathan (1976), p. 519.
41. Ramanathan (1976), p. 519.
42. Crane and Matten (2010), p. 212.
43. Crane and Matten (2010).
44. Ernst and Young (2012).
45. Global Reporting Initiative (2014b).
46. Global Reporting Initiative (2014b).
47. Global Reporting Initiative (2013).
48. Global Reporting Initiative (2013).
49. Thurm (2010).
50. Global Reporting Initiative (2013), p. 3.
51. Thurm (2010).
52. Deutsche Vereinigung für Finanzanalyse und Asset Management; DVFA.
53. DVFA (2012).
54. Schäfer, Kröner, and Seeberg (2011).
55. DVFA and EFFAS (2010).
56. Schäfer, Kröner, and Seeberg (2011).
57. Savitz and Weber (2006), p. xiii.
58. Müller (2012).
59. Schulze and Thomas (2012).
60. Schulze and Thomas (2012).
61. Internationaler Controller Verein (2010).
62. Savitz and Weber (2006), p. xiii.
63. Schwerk (2012).
64. Ziegenbein (2007).
65. Porter and Kramer (2006).
66. Carroll (1979).

67. Porter and Kramer (2011), p. 4.
68. Porter and Kramer (2011), p. 7.
69. Porter and Kramer (2002), p. 7.
70. Porter and Kramer (2011), p. 4.
71. Porter and Kramer (2011), p. 4.
72. Porter and Kramer (2011).
73. Prahalad (2010).
74. Porter and Kramer (2006).
75. Porter and Kramer (2006).
76. Porter and Kramer (2011), p. 17.
77. Porter and Kramer (2006).
78. Porter and Kramer (2011), p. 4.
79. Porter and Kramer (2011), p. 16.
80. Porter and Kramer (2011), p. 16.
81. Carroll (1979), p. 500.
82. Carroll (1979), p. 501.
83. Carroll (1979), p. 501.
84. Carroll, (1979), p. 502, following Wilson (1975).
85. Carroll (1979), p. 504.
86. Schreck (2012).
87. Raghubir, Roberts, Lemon, and Winer (2010), p. 69, taking a study of Margolis, Elfenbein, and Walsh (2007) into account.
88. Waddock and Graves (1997).
89. Carroll (1979).

Chapter 5

1. Hamel (2009), p. 91.
2. Hamel (2009), p. 91.
3. Eschenbach and Siller (2009).
4. Eschenbach and Siller (2009).
5. Eschenbach and Siller (2009).

Chapter 6

1. Bonhoeffer (2011).
2. Ernst and Young (2012).
3. Lubin and Esty (2010), p. 50.
4. Bonhoeffer (2011).
5. Eschenbach and Siller (2009).

6. Eschenbach and Siller (2009), p. 58; translated.
7. Eschenbach and Siller (2009).
8. Suchanek (2012).
9. Müller (2012).
10. Müller (2012).
11. Lubin and Esty (2010), p. 50.
12. Gill, (2006), p. 120.
13. Bamford and West (2010), p. 62.
14. Gill (2006), p. 121.
15. Gill (2006), p. 121.
16. Internationaler Controller Verein (2011).
17. Werther and Chandler (2011).
18. Carroll (1987), p. 14.
19. Carroll (1987), p. 14.
20. Carroll (1987), p. 14.
21. Jones (1991).
22. Jones (1991).
23. Jones (1991).
24. Ethics Resource Center (2012).
25. Mund (2009).
26. Ulrich (2008a).
27. Ulrich (2008a).
28. Weber and Schäffer (2000).
29. Ulrich (2008a).
30. Ulrich (2008a), p. 89.
31. Ulrich (2008a), p. 89.
32. Ulrich (2008a), p. 90.
33. Ulrich (2008a), p. 90.
34. Weber and Schäffer (2000).
35. United Nations (2000).
36. Kant (1785), p. 29.
37. Kant (1785).
38. Kant (1785), p. 29.
39. Ulrich (2008a).

Chapter 7

1. Drucker (2007), p. 56.
2. Global Reporting Initiative (2014a).
3. Global Reporting Initiative (2014a).
4. Global Reporting Initiative (2014a).

5. Mitchell, Agle, and Wood (1997).

6. Mitchell, Agle, and Wood (1997), p. 873.

7. Thielemann and Wettstein (2008), p. 37.

8. Friedman (1962), p. 133.

9. Freeman (1984), p. 46.

10. Ulrich (2008a).

11. Schulze and Thomas (2012).

12. Drucker (2007), p. 56.

13. Global Reporting Initiative (2013), p. 7.

14. Global Reporting Initiative (2013), p. 7.

15. Global Reporting Initiative (2013), p. 71.

16. Kiron, Kruschwitz, Haanaes, and von Streng Velken (2012), p. 73.

17. Global Reporting Initiative (2013).

18. Global Reporting Initiative (2013).

19. Müller (2012).

20. Attention: HR in this context must not be confused with *human resources*.

21. Willard (2014).

22. Schulz (2012).

Chapter 8

1. Author's own citation, referring to Hamel (2009), p. 91.

2. Ulrich (2008a), p. 71.

3. Kaplan and Norton (1996), p. 21.

4. United Nations (1992).

5. Schneider (2012).

6. Ulrich (2010), p. 110.

7. Thielemann and Wettstein (2008), p. 45.

8. Albert Einstein, as cited in Everett, Johnson, and Madden (2012).

References

Alternative Bank Switzerland. 2014. http://www.abs.ch/ (retrieved March 3, 2014).

Anthony, R.N. 1965. *Planning and Control Systems: A Framework for Analysis.* Boston: Division of Research, Graduate School of Business Administration, Harvard University.

Bachmann, P.J. 2011. "Nachhaltig richtig managen: die 13 Erfolgsfaktoren einer Nachhaltigkeitsstrategie." *Ernst & Young CCaSS News* 16, pp. 24–29.

Baier, P. 2008. Praxishandbuch Controlling—Controlling-Instrumente, Unter nehmensplanung und Reporting (2. updated ed.). München: mi-Fachverlag, FinanzBuch Verlag GmbH.

Bamford, C.E., and G.P. West. 2010. *Strategic Management—Value Creation, Sustainability, and Performance.* Mason: South-Western Cengage Learning.

Barbier, E.B. 1987. "The Concept of Sustainable Economic Development." *Environmental Conservation* 14, no. 2, pp. 101–110.

Baum, H.G., A.G. Coenenberg, and T. Günther. 2007. *Strategisches Controlling.* 4th ed. Stuttgart: Schäffer-Poeschel Verlag.

Beckers, B. 2010. *Controlling: Berufsfeldanalyse Deutschland und USA.* Hamburg: IGEL Verlag GmbH.

Bonhoeffer, D. 2011. *Letters & Papers from Prison—New Greatly Enlarged Edition.* New York, NY: Simon & Schuster Inc.

BP. 2012. *Upstream Investor Days.* bp.com: http://www.bp.com/content/dam/bp/pdf/investors/IC_group_overview.pdf (retrieved March 3, 2014).

Buchholz, L. 2009. *Strategisches Controlling: Grundlagen—Instrumente—Konzepte.* Wiesbaden: Gaber | GWV Fachverlage GmbH.

Cambridge University Press. 2014. *Bottom Line.* Cambridge Dictionaries Online: http://dictionary.cambridge.org/es/diccionario/ingles-americano/bottom-line_1?q=bottom+line (retrieved April 7, 2014).

Carlowitz, H.C. 2009. *Die Ökonomie der Waldkultur—Sylvicultura Oeconomica,* Reprint of the 2nd ed. of 1732. Remagen-Oberwinter.

Carroll, A.B. 1979. "A Three-Dimensional Conceptual Model of Corporate Performance." *The Academy of Management Review,* 4, no. 4, pp. 497–505.

Carroll, A.B. 1987. "In Search of the Moral Manager." *Business Horizons,* 30, no. 2, pp. 7–15.

Carroll, A.B. 2004. "Managing Ethically with Global Stakeholders: A Present and Future Challenge." *The Academy of Management Executive,* 18, no. 2, pp. 114–120.

Commission of the European Communities. 2001. GREEN PAPER—Promoting a European framework for Corporate Social Responsibility—COM(2001) 366 final. Brussels.

CONTROLLING-Portal.de. 2014. *Kennzahlen-Systeme.* CONTROLLING-Portal.de: http://www.controllingportal.de/Fachinfo/Kennzahlen/Kennzah len-Systeme.html (retrieved January 15, 2014).

Crane, A. and D. Matten. 2010. *Business ethics—Managing Corporate Citizenship and Sustainability in the Age of Globalization.* 3rd ed. Oxford: Oxford University Press.

David, J.E. 2013. *'Beyond Petroleum' No More? BP Goes Back to Basics.* CNBC—Green: http://www.cnbc.com/id/100647034 (retrieved March 3, 2014).

Deutsch, N., L. Krüger, and T. Michel. 2012. "Benchmarking als Teil eines Energiecontrollings." In *Nachhaltigkeitscontrolling—Konzepte, Instrumente und Fallbeispiele zur Umsetzung,* eds. R. Gleich, P. Bartels, and V. Breisig, pp. 141–160. Freiburg: Haufe-Lexware GmbH & Co. KG.

Drucker, P.F. 2007. *The Practice of Management.* 2nd ed. Oxford: Butterworth-Heinemann.

Drucker, P.F. 2012. *Management—Tasks, Responsibilities, Practices. reprinted ed.* Oxford: Butterworth-Heinemann.

DVFA and EFFAS. 2010. *KPIs for ESG.* EFFAS Commission On ESG: http://www.effas-esg.com/?page_id=206 (retrieved December 8, 2012).

DVFA. 2012. *Kommission Responsible Investing.* DVFA: http://www.dvfa.de/die_dvfa/kommissionen/non_financials/dok/35683.php (retrieved December 8, 2012).

EBEN—European Business Ethics Network. 2014. *eben—European Business Ethics Network.* www.eben-net.org (retrieved May 15, 2014).

Economy for the Common Good. 2013. *Economy for the Common Good—An economic model for the future.* www.gemeinwohl-oekonomie.org/en/ (retrieved March 3, 2014).

Elkington, J. 1998. *Cannibals with Forks: The Triple Bottom Line of 21st Century Business.* Gabriola Island: New Society Publishers.

Englisch, P., K. Sahr, C. Volkmann, C. Blank, and K.O. Tokarski. 2012. *Nachhaltige Unternehmensführung—Lage und aktuelle Entwicklungen im Mittelstand.* (Ernst & Young GmbH, Schumpeter School of Business and Economics, & Berner Fachhochschule, eds.) Ernst & Young.

Ernst and Young. 2012. *Six growing trends in corporate sustainability.* Ernst & Young: http://www.ey.com/Publication/vwLUAssets/Six_growing/$FILE/Six Trends.pdf (retrieved September 21, 2012).

Eschenbach, R., and H. Siller. 2009. *Controlling professionell—Konzeption und Werkzeuge.* Schäffer-Poeschel Verlag: Stuttgart.

Ethics Resource Center. 2012. "PLUS: The Decision Making Process." *Ethics Resource Center—Resources*, http://www.ethics.org/resource/plus-decision-making-process (retrieved December 19, 2012).

European Commission. 2011. Communication from the Commission to the European Parliament, the Council, the European Economic and Social Committee and the Committee of the Regions—A Renewed EU Strategy 2011–2014 for Corporate Social Responsibility—COM(2011) 681 final. Brussels.

Evan, W.M., and R.E. Freeman. 1993. "A stakeholder theory of the modern corporation: Kantian capitalism." In *Business Ethics: Readings and Cases in Corporate Morality*, eds. W.M. Hoffman, and R.E. Frederick. pp. 145–154. New York, NY: McGraw-Hill.

Everett, R.E., D.R. Johnson, and B.W. Madden. 2012. *Financial Accounting for School Administrators: Tools for Schools*. 3rd ed. Lanham: Rowman & Littlefield Education.

Fenner, D. 2008. *Ethik—Wie soll ich handeln?* Tübingen: A. Franke Verlag.

Freeman, R.E. 1984. *Strategic Management: A Stakeholder Approach*. Boston: Pitman Publishing.

Friedman, M. 1962. *Capitalism and Freedom*. Chicago: University of Chicago Press.

Friedman, M. 1970. *The Social Responsibility of Business is to Increase its Profits*. New York, NY: The New York Times Magazine.

Gälweiler, A. 2005. *Strategische Unternehmensführung*. 3rd ed. Frankfurt/Main: Campus Verlag GmbH.

Garriga, E., and D. Melé. 2004. "Corporate Social Responsibility Theories: Mapping the Territory." *Journal of Business Ethics*, 53, no. 1–2, pp. 51–71.

Gastinger, K., and P. Gaggl. 2012. "CSR als strategischer Managementansatz." In *Corporate Social Responsibility—Verantwortungsvolle Unternehmensführung in Theorie und Praxis*. eds. A. Schneider and R. Schmidpeter, pp. 241–258. Berlin Heidelberg: Springer-Verlag.

Gill, R. 2006. *Theory and Practice of Leadership*. London: SAGE Publications Ltd.

Gladen, W. 2011. *Performance Measurement—Controlling mit Kennzahlen*. 5th ed. Wiesbaden: Gabler Verlag | Springer Fachmedien.

Global Footprint Network. 2014. *Global Footprint Network—Advancing the Science of Sustainability*. www.footprintnetwork.org (retrieved March 6, 2014).

Global Reporting Initiative. 2013. *Sustainability Reporting Guidelines—G4—Reporting Principles and Standard Disclosures*. Global Reporting Initiative: https://www.globalreporting.org/resourcelibrary/GRIG4-Part1-Reporting-Principles-and-Standard-Disclosures.pdf (retrieved January 24, 2014).

Global Reporting Initiative. 2014a. G4 Online—Completeness. Global Reporting Initiative: https://g4.globalreporting.org/how-you-should-report/

reporting-principles/principles-for-defining-report-content/completeness/ Pages/default.aspx (retrieved February 6, 2014).

Global Reporting Initiative. 2014b. *What is GRI?* Global Reporting Initiative: https://www.globalreporting.org/information/about-gri/what-is-GRI/Pages/ default.aspx (retrieved January 24, 2014).

Goodpaster, K.E. 1991. "Business Ethics and Stakeholder Analysis." *Business Ethics Quarterly*, 1, no. 1, pp. 53–73.

Günther, E., and K. Stechemesser. 2011. *Instrumente des Green Controllings: ein Blick zurück ein Blick nach vorn.* Controlling—Zeitschrift für erfolgsorientierte Unternehmensführung, 23, pp. 417–423.

Gutenberg, E. 1958. *Einführung in die Betriebswirtschaftslehre.* Wiesbaden: Gabler Verlag.

Hamel, G. 2009. "Moon Shots for Management—What great challenges must we tackle to reinvent management and make it more relevant to a volatile world?" *Harvard Business Review*, 87, no. 2, pp. 91–98.

Handelsgesetzbuch. 2005. *Handelsgesetzbuch.* 43rd ed. München: Deutscher Taschenbuch Verlag GmbH & Co. KG.

Hemel, U. 2011. *Ökocontrolling vor dem Hintergrund einer werteorientierten Unternehmenssteuerung.* Controlling—Zeitschrift für erfolgsorientierte Unternehmenssteuerung, 23, pp. 412–416.

Horváth, P. 2006. *Controlling.* 10th ed. München: Verlag Franz Vahlen GmbH.

Horváth, P., J. Isensee, J, and U. Michel. 2012. "Green Controlling"—Bedarf einer Integration von ökologischen Aspekten in das Controlling. In *Integriertes Umweltcontrolling—Von der Stoffstromanalyse zum Bewertungs-und Informationssystem* 2nd ed. pp. 41–50. M. Tschandl and A. Posch (eds.), Wiesbaden: Gabler Verlag—Springer Fachmedien Wiesbaden GmbH.

Institute of Management Accountants. 2012. *Management Accounting.* IMA: http://www.imanet.org/mgi/Management_Accounting.aspx (retrieved November 23, 2012).

International Group of Controlling. 2012. *Controlling Process Model—A Guideline for Describing and Designing Controlling Processes.* (International Group of Controlling, and Horváth & Partners Management Consultants, eds.) Freiburg: Haufe.

International Group of Controlling. 2013. "Mission Statement Controller." *International Group of Controlling.* http://www.igc-controlling.org/EN/_ leitbild/leitbild.php (retrieved December 27, 2013).

International Organization for Standardization. 2010. "ISO 26000:2010(en) — Guidance on social responsibility." *ISO—Online Browsing Platform (OBP)* https://www.iso.org/obp/ui/#iso:std:iso:26000:ed-1:v1:en (retrieved October 20, 2012).

Internationaler Controller Verein. 2010. "ICV Dream Car Green Controlling—Relevanz und Ansätze einer "Begrünung" des Controlling-

Systems." *Internationaler Controller Verein—Ideenwerkstatt.* http://www. controllerverein.com/Green_Controlling.173094.html (retrieved December 5, 2012).

Internationaler Controller Verein. 2011. "ICV Studie Green Controlling—eine (neue) Herausforderung für den Controller?" *Internationaler Controller Verein— Ideenwerkstatt.* http://www.controllerverein.com/Green_Controlling.173094 .html (retrieved December 5, 2012).

Internationaler Controller Verein. 2014. "Awards." *Internationaler Controller Verein.* http://www.controllerverein.com/Archiv.293.html#Green%20 Controlling-Preis%202013 (retrieved March 6, 2014).

Internationaler Controller Verein e.V. 2002. "Controller Leitbild." *Internationaler Controller Verein—Was ist Controlling?* http://www.controllerverein.com/ Was-ist-Controlling-.50.html (retrieved November 18, 2012).

Jasch, C. 2012. *CSR und Berichterstattung.* In *Corporate Social Responsibility— Verantwortungsvolle Unternehmensführung in Theorie und Praxis,* eds. A. Schneider and R. Schmidpeter, pp. 501–512. Berlin Heidelberg: Springer-Verlag.

Jones, T.M. 1991. "Ethical Decision Making by Individuals in Organizations: An Issue-Contingent Model." *Academy of Management Review,* 16, no. 2, pp. 366–395.

Jorberg, T. 2010. "Wirtschaft von Grund auf anders lernen." *Ernst & Young CCaSS News,* 14, pp. 42–43.

Kant, I. 1785. "Groundwork for the Metaphysics of Morals" (amended by Jonathan Bennett; 2008). *Early Modern Texts.* http://www.earlymoderntexts. com/pdf/kantgrou.pdf (retrieved October 30, 2012).

Kaplan, R.S., and D.P. Norton. 1996. *The Balanced Scorecard—Translating Strategy into Action.* Boston: Harvard Business Press.

Kersten, W., J. Becker, C. Allonas, and S. Berlin. 2011. "Entwicklung von grünen Logistikdienstleistungen mit einem erweiterten Target Costing Ansatz." *Controlling—Zeitschrift für erfolgsorientierte Unternehmensführung,* 23, pp. 443–450.

Kiron, D., N. Kruschwitz, K. Haanaes, and I. von Streng Velken. 2012. "Sustainability Nears a Tipping Point." *MIT Sloan Management Review,* 53, no. 2, pp. 68–78.

KPMG. 2012. *Expect the Unexpected: Building business value in a changing world.* KPMG International Cooperative.

Kuhn, L. 2008. *Triple Bottom Line?* Harvard Business Manager, p. 12.

Lotter, D., and J. Braun. 2010. *Der CSR-Manager—Unternehmensverantwortung in der Praxis.* 1st ed. München: Altop Verlags- und Vertriebsgesellschaft mbH.

Lubin, D.A. and D.C. Esty. 2010. "The Sustainability Imperative." *Harvard Business Review,* 88, no. 5, pp. 42–50.

Mandal, S.K. 2010. *Ethics in Business and Corporate Governance.* New Delhi: Tata McGraw Hill Education Private Limited.

Margolis, J.D., H.A. Elfenbein, and J.P. Walsh. 2007. "Does It Pay to be Good?" *A meta-analysis and redirection of research on the relationship between corporate social and financial performance.* http://stakeholder.bu.edu/Docs/Walsh,%20Jim%20Does%20It%20Pay%20to%20Be%20Good.pdf (retrieved December 11, 2012).

Maxwell, J.C. 2003. *Leadership Promises for Every Day.* Nashville: Thomas Nelson, Inc.

Meadows, D., D. Meadows, E. Zahn, and P. Milling. 1972. *Die Grenzen des Wachstums—Bericht des Club of Rome zur Lage der Menschheit.* Stuttgart: Deutsche Verlags-Anstalt GmbH.

Michel, U. 2011. "Entwicklungstrends und Excellence im Controlling." In *Exzellentes Controlling, exzellente Unternehmensleistung—Best Practice und Trends im Controlling,* eds. P. Horváth, pp. 3–21. Stuttgart: Schäffer-Poeschel Verlag.

Mitchell, R.K., B.R. Agle, and D.J. Wood. 1997. "Toward a Theory of Stakeholder Identification and Salience: Defining the Principle of Who and What Really Counts." *The Academy of Management Review,* 22, no. 4, pp. 853–886. Retrieved from http://www.jstor.org/stable/259247

Müller, A. 2011. *Umweltorientierte Kostenrechnungssysteme.* Controlling—Zeitschrift für erfolgsorientierte Unternehmensführung. 23, pp. 424–429.

Müller, A. 2012. "Ansätze und Instrumente des Nachhaltigkeitscontrollings—ein praxisorientierter Überblick." In *Nachhaltigkeitscontrolling—Konzepte, Instrumente und Fallbeispiele zur Umsetzung,* eds. R. Gleich, P. Bartels, and V. Breisig, pp. 67–90. Freiburg: Haufe-Lexware GmbH & Co. KG.

Mund, A. 2009. *Controlling in mittelständischen Unternehmen.* Hamburg: IGEL Verlag GmbH.

Mutafelija, B., and H. Stromberg. 2003. *Systematic Process Improvement Using ISO 9001:2000 and CMMI.* Norwood: Artech House, Inc.

Oxford University Press. 2012a. "Dictionary—Philanthropy." *Oxford Dictionaries—The world's most trusted dictionaries.* http://oxforddictionaries.com/definition/english/philanthropy (retrieved October 20, 2012).

Oxford University Press. 2012b. "Dictionary—Responsible." *Oxford Dictionaries—The world's most trusted dictionaries.* http://oxforddictionaries.com/definition/american_english/responsible?q=responsible (retrieved October 20, 2012).

Oxford University Press. 2013. "Dictionary—Business Case." *Oxford Dictionaries—The world's most trusted dictionaries* http://www.oxforddictionaries.com/definition/english/business-case?q=business+case (retrieved December 10, 2013).

Pezzey, J. 1997. "Sustainability constraints versus 'optimality' versus intertemporal concern, and axioms versus data." *Land Economics,* 73, no. 4, pp. 448–466.

Porter, M.E., and M.R. Kramer. 2002. *The Competitive Advantage of Corporate Philanthropy.* Harvard Business Review (Reprint R0212D), pp. 5–16.

Porter, M.E., and M.R. Kramer. 2006. *Strategy and Society: The Link Between Competitive Advantage and Corporate Social Responsibility.* Harvard Business Review, pp. 78–93.

Porter, M.E., and M.R. Kramer. 2011. "Creating Shared Value—How to Reinvent Capitalism—and Unleash a Wave of Innovation and Growth." *Harvard Business Review* (Reprint R1101C), pp. 1–17.

Prahalad, C.K. 2010. *The Fortune at the Bottom of the Pyramid: Eradicating Poverty through Profits.* 5th anniversary ed. Upper Saddle River: Pearson Education, Inc.

Preißler, P.R. 2007. *Controlling—Lehrbuch und Intensivkurs* 13rd ed. München: Oldenbourg Wissenschaftsverlag GmbH.

Prengel, R. 2012. "Effizient gestaltetes Carbon Accounting verbessert Unterstützung der Stakeholder." In *Nachhaltigkeitscontrolling—Konzepte, Instrumente und Fallbeispiele zur Umsetzung,* eds. R. Gleich, P. Bartels, and V. Breisig, pp. 181–194. Freiburg: Haufe-Lexware GmbH & Co. KG.

Raghubir, P., J. Roberts, K.N. Lemon, R.S. Winer. 2010. "Why, When, and How Should the Effect of Marketing Be Measured? A Stakeholder Perspective for Corporate Social Responsibility Metrics." *Journal of Public Policy & Marketing,* 29, no. 1, pp. 66–77.

Ramanathan, K.V. 1976. "Toward A Theory of Corporate Social Accounting." *The Accounting Review,* 51, no. 3, pp. 516–528.

Reichmann, T., and M. Kißler. 2010. "Sustainability-Controlling." *Controlling—Zeitschrift für erfolgsorientierte Unternehmensführung,* 22, no. 2, pp. 104–106.

Rickards, R.C. 2007. *Budgetplanung kompakt.* München: Oldenbourg Wissenschaftsverlag GmbH.

Ries, A., and K. Wehrum. 2011. "Determinanten eines integrativen Nachhaltigkeitsmanagements und -controllings." *Controller Magazin,* 2, pp. 26–30.

Ruggie, J. 2008. "Protect, Respect and Remedy: a Framework for Business and Human Rights." *Business & Human Rights Resource Center,* http://www.business-humanrights.org/Documents/RuggieHRC2008 (retrieved December 20, 2012).

Russ, T. 2010. *Sustainability and Design Ethics.* Boca Raton: CRC Press—Taylor & Francis Group.

Savitz, A.W., and K. Weber. 2006. *The Triple Bottom Line: How Today's Best-Run Companies Are Achieving Economic, Social and Environmental Success—and How You Can Too.* San Francisco: Jossey-Bass.

Schäfer, H., F. Kröner, and B. Seeberg. 2011. "Zielgruppengerechte Nachhaltigkeitsberichterstattung mit Hilfe des Socially Responsible Investment (SRI)-Factsheets." *Controlling—Zeitschrift für erfolgsorientierte Unternehmensführung,* 23, pp. 466–472.

Schäffer, U., and J. Weber. 2005. *Bereichscontrolling—Funktionsspezifische Anwendungsfelder, Methoden und Instrumente,* eds. U. Schäffer, and J. Weber. Stuttgart: Schäffer-Poeschel Verlag.

Schaltegger, S., S.E. Windolph, and D. Harms. 2010. *Corporate Sustainability Barometer—Wie nachhaltig agieren Unternehmen in Deutschland?* London: PricewaterhouseCoopers.

Schneider, A. 2012. "Reifegradmodell CSR—eine Begriffserklärung und -abgrenzung." In *Corporate Social Responsibility—Verantwortungsvolle Unternehmensführung in Theorie und Praxis*, eds. A. Schneider, and R. Schmidpeter, pp. 17–38. Berlin Heidelberg: Springer-Verlag.

Schreck, P. 2012. "Der Business Case for Corporate Social Responsibility." In *Corporate Social Responsibility—Verantwortungsvolle Unternehmensführung in Theorie und Praxis*, eds. A. Schneider and R. Schmidpeter, pp. 67–86. Berlin Heidelberg: Springer-Verlag.

Schulz, O. 2012. "Nachhaltige ganzheitliche Wertschöpfungsketten." In *Corporate Social Responsibility—Verantwortungsvolle Unternehmensführung in Theorie und Praxis*, eds. A. Schneider and R. Schmidpeter, pp. 271–284. Berlin Heidelberg: Springer-Verlag.

Schulze, M., and S. Thomas. 2012. "Strategisches Nachhaltigkeits-Controlling bei der Deutschen Telekom AG." *Controller Magazin*, pp. 58–63.

Schwerk, A. 2012. "Strategische Einbettung von CSR in das Unternehmen." In *Corporate Social Responsibility—Verantwortungsvolle Unternehmensführung in Theorie und Praxis*, eds. A. Schneider and R. Schmidpeter, pp. 329–356. Berlin Heidelberg: Springer-Verlag.

Smith, A., and Playfair, W. 1811. *An Inquiry into the Nature and Causes of the Wealth of Nations*. Hartford: Peter B. Gleason & Co. Printers.

Society for Business Ethics. 2014. *Society for Business Ethics.* www.sbeonline.org (retrieved May 16, 2014).

Stabenow, S. 2010. "Pioniere der Nachhaltigkeit: Dennis L. Meadows." *Ernst & Young CCaSS News* 14, pp. 46–47.

Suchanek, A. 2012. "Vertrauen als Grundlage nachhaltiger unternehmerischer Wertschöpfung." In *Corporate Social Responsibility—Verantwortungsvolle Unternehmensführung in Theorie und Praxis*, eds. A. Schneider and R. Schmidpeter, pp. 55–66. Berlin Heidelberg: Springer-Verlag.

Thielemann, U. 2010. System Error—Warum der freie Markt zur Unfreiheit führt. (Bundeszentrale für politische Bildung, Ed.) Bonn: Westend Verlag Frankfurt/Main in der Piper Verlag GmbH.

Thielemann, U., and F. Wettstein. 2008. The Case against the Business Case and the Idea of "Earned Reputation". Discussion Papers of the Institute for Business Ethics(111). MeM – Denkfabrik für Wirtschaftsethik: http://www.mem-wirtschaftsethik.de/das-mem/publikationen/the-case-against-the-business-case/ (retrieved December 15, 2012).

Thurm, R. 2010. Sustainability Reporting 2.0: from 'Trojan horse' to 'value booster.' In *Responsible Business—How to Manage a CSR Strategy Successfully,* eds. M. Pohl, and N. Tolhurst, pp. 107–128. Chichester: John Wiley & Sons Ltd.

Tschandl, M. 2012. Perspektiven der Integration im Umweltcontrolling. In *Integriertes Umweltcontrolling—Von der Stoffstromanalyse zum Bewertungs- und Informationssystem*, eds. M. Tschandl, and A. Posch, pp. 11–39. 2nd ed. Wiesbaden: Gabler Verlag—Springer Fachmedien Wiesbaden GmbH.

Tschandl, M., and Posch, A. 2012. Preface. In *Integriertes Umweltcontrolling— Von der Stoffstromanalyse zum Bewertungs- und Informationssystem*. eds. M. Tschandl, and A. Posch. pp. 5–6. 2nd ed. Wiesbaden: Gabler Verlag— Springer Fachmedien Wiesbaden GmbH.

Ulrich, P. 2008a. *Integrative Economic Ethics—Foundations of a Civilized Market Economy*. Cambridge: University Press.

Ulrich, P. 2008b. *Integrative Wirtschaftsethik—Grundlagen einer lebensdienlichen Ökonomie* (4th completely revised ed.). Bern—Stuttgart—Wien: Haupt Verlag.

Ulrich, P. 2010. "Civilizing the Market Economy: The Approach of Integrative Economic Ethics to Sustainable Development." *Economics, Management & Financial Markets*, 1, pp. 99–112.

United Nations. 1987. Report of the World Commission on Environment and Development—A/RES/42/187.   http://www.un.org/documents/ga/res/42/ares42-187.htm (retrieved October 21, 2012).

United Nations. 1992. Rio Declaration on Environment and Development—A/ CONF.151/26   (Vol.   I).   http://www.un.org/documents/ga/conf151/aconf15126-1annex1.htm (retrieved October 21, 2012).

United Nations. 2000. "The Ten Principles." *United Nations Global Compact* http://www.unglobalcompact.org/AboutTheGC/TheTenPrinciples/index.html (retrieved September 22, 2012).

United Nations. 2010, 2011. "World Population Prospects, the 2010 Revision." *United Nations, Department of Economic and Social Affairs*. http://esa.un.org/unpd/wpp/Analytical-Figures/htm/fig_13.htm (retrieved September 22, 2012).

United Nations. 2012. *The Universal Declaration of Human Rights—Full Text*. United Nations, http://www.un.org/en/documents/udhr/ (retrieved December 20, 2012).

van Marrewijk, M. 2003. "Concepts and Definitions of CSR and Corporate Sustainability: Between Agency and Communion." *Journal of Business Ethics*, 44 (2/3, Corporate Sustainability Conference 2002: The Impact of CSR on Management Disciplines), pp. 95–105.

Vaude. 2013. "Sustainability Report 2013." *Vaude—Responsibility*, http://www.vaude.com/en-GB/Responsibility/Sustainability-Report/ (retrieved March 3, 2014).

Waddock, S.A., and S.B. Graves. 1997. "The Corporate Social Performance-Financial Performance Link." *Strategic Management Journal*, 18, no. 4, pp. 303–319.

Weber, J., and U. Schäffer. 2000. *Balanced Scorecard & Controlling* 3rd ed. Wiesbaden: Gabler Verlag.

Weber, J., J. Georg, R. Janke, and S. Mack. 2012. *Nachhaltigkeit und Controlling*. 1st ed. Vol. 80 Advanced Controlling. Weinheim: Wiley-VCH Verlag GmbH & Co. KGaA.

Weissmann, F. 2005. *Unternehmen steuern mit Controlling—Leitfaden und Toolbox für die Praxis*. Berlin—Heidelberg: Springer Verlag.

Werther, W.B., and D. Chandler. 2011. *Strategic Corporate Social Responsibility—Stakeholders in a Global Environment*. 2nd ed. Thousand Oaks: SAGE Publications, Inc.

Wilde, O. 2009. "The Picture of Dorian Gray." *Kaye Dreams Novel Art*. http://books.google.de/books?id=6h3mT8-eTI4C&printsec=frontcover&dq=The+Picture+of+Dorian+Gray&hl=de&sa=X&ei=rXwUU8amGIrYtAaLq4CIBA&ved=0CDwQ6AEwAA#v=onepage&q=nowadays%20people&f=false (retrieved March 3, 2014).

Willard, B. 2012. *The New Sustainability Advantage—Seven Business Case Benefits of a Triple Bottom Line*. Gabriola Island: New Society Publishers.

Willard, B. 2014. "Sustainability Advantage Worksheets—About." *Sustainability Advantage (TM)*. http://sustainabilityadvantage.com/products/worksheets.html (retrieved March 7, 2014).

Wilson, I. 1975. "What one company is doing about today's demands on business." In *Changing business-society interrelationships*, ed. G.A. Steiner, pp. 121–140. Los Angeles: Graduate School of Management, UCLA.

Wöhe, G., and U. Döring. 2010. *Einführung in die Allgemeine Betriebswirtschaftslehre*. 24th revised and updated ed. München: Vahlen Verlag.

Ziegenbein, K. 2007. *Controlling*. 9th revised and updated, ed. K. Olfert. Ludwigshafen (Rhein): Friedrich Kiehl Verlag GmbH.

Index

This book is a publication in support of the United Nations Principles for Responsible Management Education (PRME), housed in the UN Global Compact Office. The mission of the PRME initiative is to inspire and champion responsible management education, research and thought leadership globally. Please visit www.unprme.org for more information.

The Principles for Responsible Management Education Book Collection is edited through the Center for Responsible Management Education (CRME), a global facilitator for responsible management education and for the individuals and organizations educating responsible managers. Please visit www.responsiblemanagement.net for more information.

—Oliver Laasch, University of Manchester, Collection Editor

- *Business Integrity in Practice: Insights from International Case Studies* by Agata Stachowicz-Stanusch and Wolfgang Amann
- *Academic Ethos Management: Building the Foundation for Integrity in Management Education* by Agata Stachowicz-Stanusch
- *Responsible Management: Understanding Human Nature, Ethics, and Sustainability* by Kemi Ogunyemi
- *Fostering Spirituality in the Workplace: A Leader's Guide to Sustainability* by Priscilla Berry
- *A Practical Guide to Educating for Responsibility in Management and Business* by Ross McDonald
- *Educating for Values-Driven Leadership: Giving Voice to Values Across the Curriculum* by Mary Gentile, Editor (with 14 contributing authors)
- *Teaching Anticorruption: Developing a Foundation for Business Integrity* by Agata Stachowicz-Stanusch and Hans Krause Hansen
- *Corporate Social Responsibility: A Strategic Perspective* by David Chandler
- *Teaching Ethics Across the Management Curriculum: A Handbook for International Faculty* by Kemi Ogunyemi

Announcing the Business Expert Press Digital Library

Concise e-books business students need for classroom and research

This book can also be purchased in an e-book collection by your library as

- a one-time purchase,
- that is owned forever,
- allows for simultaneous readers,
- has no restrictions on printing, and
- can be downloaded as PDFs from within the library community.

Our digital library collections are a great solution to beat the rising cost of textbooks. E-books can be loaded into their course management systems or onto students' e-book readers.

The **Business Expert Press** digital libraries are very affordable, with no obligation to buy in future years. For more information, please visit **www.businessexpertpress.com/librarians**. To set up a trial in the United States, please email **sales@businessexpertpress.com**.